CHRONIC DEPRESSION:
A USER'S MANUAL

Gabriel Reisinger

Gabriel Reisinger

Published by Gabriel Reisinger at Createspace

Copyright © 2016 Gabriel Reisinger

All rights reserved.

Cover Design by Lindsey Màrton

Createspace Edition, License Notes

Thank you for purchasing this book. You are welcome to share it with your friends.

This book may be reproduced, copied and distributed for non-commercial purposes, provided the book remains in its complete original form. Thank you for your support.

Table of Contents

Preface 7

What is Persistent Depressive Disorder? 12

What Does PDD Feel Like? 29

Depression Psychology 44

Depression Physiology 61

PDD and Habits: How to Identify and Change Them .. 95

Clinical Treatment 118

Coping and Self-Care 134

Resources 167

Conclusion 173

Small Thank You and About the Author 177

Notes 178

Index 182

To the late Margaret Lobenstine. Without whom I never would have undertaken this project.

This book is not intended to replace professional medical advice. If you are struggling with depression I recommend you talk to a family doctor or therapist. Use this book as a supplement to professional help. This book is current as of March 2016, and as new information becomes available some of the information in this book may become invalid. You should seek the most up-to-date information from a licensed professional.

Preface

Before you get started I want you to know a few things about me. I am not a psychiatrist or a therapist or any kind of doctor. I'm just a guy living with Persistent Depressive Disorder (PDD). I wanted to write about this particular disorder because it affects me and many other people. Most everyone has heard of depression but, I've found that many people are not aware that certain types of depression can last for years or decades.

I don't have professional experience in this field, but I've lived with PDD for at least a decade (if not longer) now. During this time I ran into a lot of people who hadn't even heard of this disease and didn't understand what I was dealing with. As a result, I was given a lot of advice

Preface

that wasn't useful and I often felt completely misunderstood. I also felt very alone as I struggled with this form of depression. Working my way through this, I wished there was material written by someone who had both had the same illness and had factual information to back up what they shared. I wanted this for myself, and I also wanted it for the people in my life who were too uninformed or misinformed to be helpful.

To be honest, I never expected to be the one to create and share such material. However, knowing others are out there in need of this information, both for themselves and for the people around you, motivated me to write what you're reading. While I don't have access to all the medical journals and information that doctors do, I've done a lot of research on the subject. PDD is a specific form of depression, and it's important to get the facts right. It's also something I deal with personally, and everything I've included, I've experienced myself and personally believe. I hope you get as much out of reading this as I did from writing it. While we may never meet in person, knowing that you're out there in need of help pushed me to get this accomplished. So I thank you whole heartedly in advance.

It may be helpful for you to know a little of my personal story. My parents separated when I was eight years old. This event in my childhood was most likely the catalyst for my depression. Not understanding what was happening to me, I became increasingly irritable and angry at the world as I got older. The emotions I was experiencing were the first symptoms of my oncoming depression. Looking back, the things that would anger me then seem trivial now. But, given my view of the world was warped by illness, the smallest things could have a big impact on my life. A specific example being I would get unreasonably annoyed when people would have their headlights on during the daytime. For some reason that bothered me even though it had zero bearing on my life.

The fact that I was ill became obvious in my senior year of high school when my appetite dwindled away to nothing. I lost a lot of weight without trying. It was a difficult time, but luckily I had a friend who recognized the symptoms as possibly depression-related and convinced me to talk to someone. I saw a few therapists over the next five or six years and slowly pulled myself out of the major depressive episode I was in. However, none of them ever mentioned the possibility of Dysthymic Disorder, and there was always this looming shadow, the feeling I was never fully cured. Sure, I felt a lot better for a time, but things still didn't seem as right as they should have been. Being the inquisitive person that I am, I began to look for a reason as to why I felt that way. Was it my personality? An illness that hadn't been properly addressed? Something else I hadn't even heard of?

Preface

Researching the issue, I came across an illness I had never heard of before: Dysthymia (This is the old name for the illness. It has been updated to Persistent Depressive Disorder in the new version of the DSM). The description matched my symptoms pretty much to a "T," and I had found my answer. But that was it, just an answer. Outside of the fact Persistent Depressive Disorder was a diagnosed condition recognized by the psychological community, there was frustratingly little information about it. What was even worse was that the general public was so unaware of the condition. PDD is hard to see in another person without being intimately aware of its specific symptoms. The disease is so subtle it can be taken as a personality trait and never treated properly.

Understanding how difficult it can be to identify PDD motivated me to bring awareness to the public about this form of depression and to help those who have it or know someone who has it. I've attempted to compile as much information about PDD as possible and present it in a way that's both easy to understand and useful. It's my goal to spread awareness about this condition generally, and specifically to let sufferers like you know you're not alone, and there is help.

As someone with PDD, I understand trying to change yourself is a tiresome and lengthy project. But, if you take your time and work on improving yourself when you have the energy to do so, I am confident you will achieve change. As you work your way through this book, the only thing I recommend is that you take your time. You didn't end up this way overnight, and you certainly won't fix it overnight either. Do the exercises and absorb the information. It will make it easier to explain what you're going through to other people, understand your treatment more fully, and implemented strategies will be more successful. So proceed with the knowledge that you can beat chronic depression and will become a stronger person from your illness.

~Gabriel Reisinger

Chapter 1
What is Persistent Depressive Disorder?

In order for you to fight this illness I think it is of the utmost importance that you understand it. A few reasons for this are as follows:

1. Knowing what the illness is and being familiar with the symptoms will allow you to decide if you have this disorder or not.

2. Knowledge about the illness will allow you to effectively fight the effects of the illness.

3. If you don't have the disorder you will be able to recognize it in others and have a better idea of what they're going through.

I cannot stress enough how important it is to become familiar with the material in this chapter. It will form the basis of the tools you will use to work on becoming healthy again. I have done my best to relay this information in a way that is relatable and comprehensive in scope. I also understand that many people do not care for dry scientific material. So, I am hoping to present the information in a way that is easy to understand while not omitting important information. Now, without further delay let's jump right in to what I hope will be the only boring part of this chapter; the clinical definition of Persistent Depressive Disorder.

There is a book in the psychology world titled Diagnostic and Statistical Manual of Mental Disorders or DSM. It is more or less the bible of psychological diagnosis and every psychologist or psychiatrist in the field uses this book. It lists very specific criteria that a person must meet in order to qualify for a mental illness. The previous version of the DSM listed Persistent Depressive Disorder only as Dysthymia (a mild chronic depression). The new version of the DSM has updated their definition and criteria of Dysthymia to include Chronic Major Depressive Disorder. This new combined disorder is called Persistent Depressive Disorder (PDD or chronic depression as I will refer to it sometimes).

What is Persistent Depressive Disorder?

Under the category of Persistent Depressive Disorder there are a few variations. Dysthymia is the milder version and Chronic Major Depressive Disorder is the more severe version. It is possible to have a depressive episode while also having chronic depression. This would only apply to Dysthymia because you can't have a major depressive episode with Chronic Major Depressive Disorder. When someone has both Dysthymia and a Major Depressive Episode it is referred to as a double depression. The determining factor for receiving a diagnosis of Dysthymia or Chronic Major Depressive Disorder is the amount of time you have had symptoms of a depressive episode.

This might seem tedious and a bit like splitting hairs. All of these slight differences are only to diagnose someone. I think something should be said for how your illness is affecting your life. I personally have had symptoms of major depression, but the symptoms I did have weren't affecting my life in a major way. This has led therapists I've talked to giving me the Dysthymic Disorder diagnoses. There can be some overlap at times and I wouldn't get too hung up on getting the perfect diagnoses. Knowing you have chronic depression of some kind (even if it isn't entirely clear which category you fall under) is going to help you move in the right direction. I believe it is also possible for your diagnoses to change from time to time. This is another reason to not worry about getting the perfect diagnoses.

The following section will outline the exact requirements from the DSM for Persistent Depressive Disorder. If you think you may have or know someone who may have Persistent Depressive Disorder do not self-diagnose them. Meeting some (or most) of the criteria listed below means you should talk to a doctor or someone in the mental health field to get a proper diagnoses. Mental health is tricky and there is a lot of overlap between some illnesses. It's vital to talk to a professional in order to rule out any other possibilities.

Requirements of Persistent Depressive Disorder

This section was taken verbatim out of the DSM and reads as follows:

A. Depressed mood for most of the day, for more days than not, as indicated by either subjective account or observation by others, for at least 2 years (1 year in adolescents or children and the mood can be expressed as irritability.)

B. Presence, while depressed, of two (or more) of the following:

1. Poor appetite or overeating.

2. Insomnia or hypersomnia.

3. Low energy or fatigue.

4. Low self-esteem.

What is Persistent Depressive Disorder?

5. Poor concentration or difficulty making decisions.

6. Feelings of hopelessness.

C. During the 2-year period (1 year for children or adolescents) of the disturbance, the individual has never been without the symptoms in Criteria A and B for more than 2 months at a time.

D. Criteria for a major depressive disorder may be continuously present for 2 years.

E. There has never been a manic episode or a hypomanic episode, and criteria have never been met for cyclothymic disorder.

F. The disturbance is not better explained by a persistent schizo affective disorder, schizophrenia, delusional disorder, or other specified or unspecified schizophrenia spectrum and other psychotic disorder.

G. The symptoms are not attributable to the physiological effects of a substance (e.g., a drug of abuse, a medication) or another medical condition (e.g. hypothyroidism).

H. The symptoms cause clinically significant distress or impairment in social, occupation, or other important areas of functioning. (1)

There are several other symptoms that can occur with depression that the DSM leaves out. They are typically seen in Major Depressive Disorder. However, personal experience and reading about other people with PDD indicated that these symptoms may be present as well.

They are as follows:

Anhedonia:

This is the symptom that makes depression so devastating. Anhedonia is the loss of the ability to feel pleasure. This is the symptom that makes people lose interest in things they used to love. Depression is (at least to my knowledge) the only illness in which this symptom is present. Understanding anhedonia clarifies why depressed people have such a hard time doing anything.

Grief/Guilt:

This can show up as obsessing about things that have happened in the past. In some cases the grief or guilt can be so severe as to cause delusions. Not the schizophrenic type of delusions you may be thinking of but, a warped perception of reality. One where the patient is unable to accept any forward progress as positive and good. There are many instances when a patient will make excuses for their positive progress (of any kind) in order to make it fit into their negative world view. This can absolutely play into other depressive symptoms as well and is one of the reasons all forms of depression are so difficult to deal with.

Self-Harm:

This is a terrible symptom of depression and many other mental illnesses. It refers to any form of self-harm including suicide. Examples of self-harm are cutting, burning, biting, or hitting one's self. I would even put drug and alcohol abuse under the self-harm category. They cause damage to the body like other self-harm acts. The difference being the distraction involved is pleasure instead of pain.

Now this doesn't mean that people who drink or use drugs (for whatever reason) are motivated by self-harm. Rather, it is the reason for which they use them. Self-harm is a coping mechanism that some people use to help them handle a variety of emotions. Healthy individuals who use these substances for recreation are not coping in a pathological way. Yes they may be causing themselves harm in the long run but, the reason for using is much different than for someone who is ill.

Self-harm can quickly become addictive and make treatment more difficult depending on how severe it is. If you or someone you know is self-harming it is imperative you seek help immediately. There is a list of resources in Chapter 8 to get help as soon as possible.

Psychomotor Retardation:

This refers to the lack of energy that one has while dealing with depression. Physical actions seem to take a huge amount of energy and everything feels exhausting. The DSM lists low energy and fatigue but, I felt it was helpful to give a clearer idea of what that might be.

When talking about this symptom it refers to the feeling that everything is simply exhausting. Feeling like you can't get out of bed or perform simple tasks are some example. It can make simple tasks feel impossible or limit your ability to accomplish more complex tasks (e.g. reading, writing, work, exercise). Along with anhedonia, psychomotor retardation can be incredibly debilitating. Quality of life severely depreciates if it progresses to the point where taking care of oneself is a chore.

As you can see this helps to paint a much clearer picture of what is and what is not Persistent Depressive Disorder. The most important determining factor in chronic depression is the length of time. Most people when they hear or think of depression imagine it as a time of grief or intense sadness. It is a period of time from several weeks up until 2 years (as per the DSM). I find that it is important to make this distinction because in my experience people are unaware that one can be depressed for years at a time. Even more critical is that episodic depression (or a depressive episode) is a different illness than chronic depression.

They share many of the same symptoms but, their causes and treatments are usually different. Episodic depression refers to when someone is going through a period of grief or hardship. People can enter a depressive state after a loved one has passed or they lost their job. They may have many of the symptoms discussed in this chapter and receive a diagnoses of depression. They key difference is that they bounce back. At some point they break their depressive cycle and are able to return to the mood state previous to the depressive trigger. These episodes also tend to last only a few weeks up to the two year limit before it becomes chronic depression. They are episodes because after a length of time symptoms disappear for longer than two months.

Chronic depression is what is described in this chapter. Persistent depressive symptoms for at least two years and have not disappeared for more than two months. I feel it is important to make this distinction because I believe these two types of depression should be treated and addressed differently. Similar to how a head cold and chest cold are colds, but they have different treatments. I think this line of thought can be applied to depression which is why I focus on chronic and not episodic depression.

It is important to familiarize yourself with the criteria and symptoms of this disorder. This will help to lessen any anxiety you may have and will help you take steps to counteract any symptoms you are experiencing.

Habits and Depression:

You may be wondering why I used the word counteract in regards to symptoms. As if we have some ability to control which symptoms we do or do not get. While we don't have much control over which symptoms we experience we do have the ability to lessen and even reverse their effects. Unlike illness with an external factor such as a virus or bacteria, many symptoms of depression are self-inflicted. Now, I must be clear in stating that you did not consciously give yourself this disease. This came about as a complex interaction of many different factors. Environment, genetics, mental health, diet, outlook on life, these are just a few of the factors that influence whether you are susceptible to depression or not. Realizing this, I began to learn about habits and how they shape our personalities.

Habits are a complex topic all on their own. They form the basis for many actions we take throughout the day in order to free up our minds for more important things. In fact we rely on habits so much that without them our brains would be on overload and we wouldn't be able to get anything done. So, why habits? Why are they so important to understanding depression? Well, to clear one thing up, habits don't necessarily apply to the person who has a depressive episode and comes out of it in a few weeks to months and is back to where they were before. Since I am talking about persistent depressive disorder, habits are actually quite important to this subset of depressive sufferers.

Of course our habits can throw us into a depressive episode. But, it's when we form new habits, while in said episode, that I believe the problems begin. There is a wide range among people for the amount of time it takes to form a habit. If you happen to be a fast learner or pick up new habits quickly, it seems like a probable possibility that you could learn negative habits as quickly as positive ones. Therefore being put into a depressed mood and then learning habits that are not conducive to reversing a depressed state would point to a person who stays depressed for a long time. Later in chapter 5 I will revisit habits and PDD in more detail.

When Symptoms Begin Matters:

You may have noticed listed under criteria C are two different lengths. One for adults and one for children or adolescents. The distinction is important because children and teens process emotions a bit differently than adults do. Subsequently they also present different symptoms of depression than adults. The main ones being irritability or anger. This makes it more difficult to diagnose properly in children and adolescents, but it also matters because the onset of the illness is important.

Chronic Depression: A User's Manual

Due to the lengthy nature of the disorder, knowing if someone was early onset (before age 21) or late onset (after the age of 21) is relevant to treatment. Not so much the type of treatment administered (although that may be affected,) but the approach used. See, those who have early onset Persistent Depressive Disorder may not even know that anything is wrong. Acquiring the illness at a young age can blur the lines between illness and your actual personality.

This is one of the more tragic parts of chronic depression. To lose who you are and become the illness. Not enough people know that this is an actual thing and go through their lives feeling out of place and not quite right. We are always told that depression is this massive event that completely turns your world upside down. I don't mean to trivialize major depressive episodes because they are a terrible experience. But, people who recover from a depressive episode have a vastly different experience of the illness. Getting stuck in the illness is something most people do not realize can happen. Without bringing awareness to this side of depression there are sick people out there who may never know they can get help. And if you've ever felt helpless in your life you know how horrible that feels.

This is the catch of the illness. While the effects of PDD are often more mild than that of a Major Depressive Episode the fact they can last (and frequently do) an entire lifetime makes it a severe disorder. It seems

What is Persistent Depressive Disorder?

counter intuitive but, people with PDD (specifically Dysthymia) commit more suicide than those with some kind of Major Depression. This is because of the psychomotor retardation symptom. People in the middle of a Major Depressive Episode literally find the idea of suicide exhausting (This is also the reason anti-depressants can cause suicide. After taking them the patient finally has the energy to do what they've wanted to for a long time).

Depression is More Than a Mental Illness:

Up until this point I have been discussing PDD as a purely mental disorder. And while there is an enormous mental component to any form of mental illness many of them also have specific physiological responses as well. Persistent Depressive Disorder is no different and when observing someone with PDD it becomes obvious that there is more than just mental trouble going on. The body is undergoing a massive stress response when dealing with any form of depression. All of the classic stress symptoms are visible:

Low Energy

Headaches

Upset stomach

Muscle aches and pains

Tense muscles

Chest pain and rapid heartbeat

Insomnia

Lowered immune response

Low sex drive or libido

Anxiety

Dry mouth

Clenched jaw and teeth grinding

All of these things can happen during depression and I'm sure all of you have experience at least one of these symptoms. While a little stress in our lives is natural and healthy, prolonged periods of stress create a host of issues. When you understand this piece of the puzzle it becomes easier to see how depression manifests itself. A traumatic event happens in a person's life which leads to heightened and lengthy stress response. This response can turn into a depressive episode and without proper treatment the mind begins to build depressive habits. These habits are what PDD is built upon. Now, as I mentioned before, simply because someone experiences a traumatic event in their life does not mean they will end up with PDD or any kind of depressive disorder for that matter. We all handle stress in different ways.

What is Persistent Depressive Disorder?

I have attempted to give a brief and informative description of what Persistent Depressive Disorder is and is not. As I mentioned in the beginning of this chapter I feel that being informed about your illness is a huge step in managing and/or riding yourself of the disease. The following chapters have more specific information pertaining to different areas of PDD. These are areas in which I feel give people the most difficulty and areas I feel are the most important in proper recovery. On the following page I have also included a short questionnaire to help you decide if you or someone you know may have PDD.

I know that this is a difficult time in your life and that many times you will not feel like doing the work necessary to make progress. That's okay. This is an illness that takes a long time to manifest itself and it will take a long time to undo. It's okay if you have a bad day, week, or month. Just remember to come back whenever you're ready and keep going. Only with persistence do we see change.

PDD Questionnaire:

If you are unsure of whether you have PDD or not this questionnaire should clarify that for you. This worksheet can also be given to someone else you suspect of having PDD as well. Think about each question and simply answer yes or no to each.

Chronic Depression: A User's Manual

1. Do you often feel "down in the dumps" or in a "bad mood" for no apparent reason?

2. Do you have a hard time falling asleep or often have thoughts that keep you up at night?

3. Do you experience fatigue during the day even when getting enough sleep?

4. Do you feel fine for short periods of time (a few days to a month or two) and then suddenly fall back into a bad mood?

5. Do you sometimes lack the motivation to do the simplest tasks?

6. Do you often have a hard time accepting compliments from others because you don't believe them?

7. Is it hard to do things you used to like because they no longer feel fulfilling or fun?

8. Have you gained or lost a significant amount of weight due to a change in eating habits?

9. Do you have thoughts of suicide or self-harm?

10. How long have you been experiencing any of the above?

If a majority of your answers are yes to questions 1-9 and more than two years for question 10 there is a good possibility that you have PDD. I recommend you speak

What is Persistent Depressive Disorder?

to a qualified professional to get a proper diagnosis and know that you are one step closer to beating your illness.

Chapter 2
What does PDD Feel Like?

This chapter will illustrate what living with PDD is like. This is not for those who have/suspect they have PDD, but for the people who think someone they know may have the disorder. If you have PDD this chapter may help you articulate your feelings to others in a way that is easier to understand. Which can be an invaluable resource. Having friends and family who understand your illness will make it easier to get help. There is also a section at the end outlining how you can go about finding a therapist if you don't already have one.

It is incredibly stressful to work through depression and not something I would wish upon anyone. It destroys lives and is not the romanticized lifestyle that some

What does PDD Feel Like?

people like to believe. 1.5% of the U.S population (approximately 4.8 million) suffers from PDD with 49.7% of those cases being classified as "severe". (2) Keep in mind that these are only numbers for adults. Remember that PDD can (and often does) start in children and adolescents. While it is a small percentage of the population it's still a large number of adults who struggle with this illness. While PDD is not as common as other types of depression it's still quite possible you know someone with this illness.

As explained in chapter 1, PDD affects every facet of your life. Your emotional and mental state suffers as well as the physical symptoms associated with depression. While you may understand or even empathize with those who have PDD, it can still be difficult to understand exactly what is going on. I'd like to try and explain what having depression feels like to those of you who have been lucky enough never to have to deal with this illness.

Depression is an illness just like any other. It isn't caused by a bacteria or virus, lack of nutrients, or lack of exercise. While it is an illness of the mind, it affects your body physically as well. The causes of depression are varied and it would be difficult to list them all. Some of these causes are biochemical imbalances, poor nutrition, another physical illness, state of mind, or a tragic life event. A person may only have one cause or sometimes multiple causes. It's also possible for depression to occur alongside other mental illnesses as well (in fact this is more often the case than not). The main thing to remember is that the cause(s) of depression are as complex as the illness itself.

Everyone has been ill at some point in their life. We all get colds, aches and pains, the occasional flu. Remember back to the last time you were sick. Your body feels run down. People typically don't feel like doing much when they are sick. We tend to lay around and/or hide from the world. Of course we all have obligations and we must work through them when we're sick, but it's not much fun and we look forward to being able to sit down and relax away from it all. Take the response you have to feeling ill and now you start to get an idea of how a person with depression feels.

Depression feels like being sick. Your body is run down and it's hard to sleep or all you want to do is sleep. Your body can be in physical pain and you don't want to socialize. Now imagine all of that and now it lasts four to eight months. Depression feels like being sick for that long. And that's just a major depressive episode. Chronic depression has all of the symptoms of a depressive episode except they last for years.

In the same way that you can't think your way out of being sick, you can't think your way out of depression either. Now, there is a lot of mental work that goes into pulling oneself out of depression. It's simply not the

What does PDD Feel Like?

same kind of "think positive" train of thought many people propagate. The human body does a wonderful job of taking care of physical invaders on its own. We don't have to put much effort into fighting off a cold. Curing (and I'm not totally convinced someone can ever be cured of chronic depression) depression takes a much longer time and more work. It takes many months of concentrated effort and analyzing one's thoughts to begin the healing process. This doesn't even include the social, nutritional, and physical work that many people with depression also require to heal.

Supporting Someone with Depression:

If you read chapter one, you know what the symptoms of PDD are and how to identify them. In this section I will go over what you can do to support someone going through this and what you can do to help. Before we begin, it is crucial to understand that helping someone with PDD is not easy. They will most likely fight you at every turn and can often times be needy and negative. This is not who that person is but simply how the disease tells the mind and body to protect itself. Years of habit building have conditioned this person to react certain ways. It is vital that you go over the terms of your help with the person you plan on helping. Having a support network greatly improves the healing process and laying out the terms of the support will help the ill person push away feelings of alienation. There is no way for me to go over the array of support possibilities within this book. It will be a very personal contract between you and the person you wish to help. Each person will differ in what they need during their treatment and it's likely that their needs will change with time. When that person is in a better place everyone involved will be better people because of it. So, don't be afraid to help someone in need, but don't take this job lightly.

Don't feel as though you need to be completely involved in that person's life. The amount of help you are willing to give is entirely up to you. Anything you can contribute will be helpful. If all you do is get them to go to a therapist and begin treatment that is a huge first step and you can feel good knowing that you've increased their chances of recovery enormously. Now, let's go over the ways that you can someone under the influence of PDD.

What to do if you know someone who has PDD:

If you have made it this far into the chapter, you may have already decided to try and help someone. There are many different things you can do to help someone with PDD and as I'm sure you've figured out by now this will be the section where I discuss some of the ways you can provide that help. Keep in mind that there is no one size fits all approach and people will respond differently to each suggestion.

What does PDD Feel Like?

Professional Help:

Unless you are someone trained in the field of mental health this is the most helpful thing you can do for someone suffering from chronic depression. A therapist can do wonders for someone who has depression. They can aid in making a proper diagnosis and find the best way to help the person in question. I cannot stress how important it is to find a therapist. They should be the foundation upon which the rest of the treatment is built.

Finding the right therapist is also important. If after a few sessions the patient and therapist don't seem to have chemistry, it's perfectly fine to look for another one. It is important that the patient likes their therapist and views them as helpful. Every therapist has their own style and way of approaching therapy. Just like finding the right dosage for a medication it can take a few tries before you find a therapist that works. The rewards are worth the effort.

Some ways you can help in this process are helping them look for a therapist, setting up appointments, and driving them to and from appointments. At first it might be difficult to get them to go and they may need an accountability partner to help motivate them to see their therapist. You are basically holding that person to their commitment to see a therapist. Depressed people (and sometimes not depressed people) may need a little push at times to help them fulfill their promises.

Know that this is a huge help and will go a long way in their treatment. If there is only one thing you can do to try and help someone, getting them to a therapist is probably the one that will have the biggest impact.

Convincing Someone They Should See a Therapist:

So you want to help someone who you think has depression. The next step is talking to them and getting them to understand that they need to seek professional help. Some people will resist help for a variety of reasons. However, know that you are helping and don't give up if they shoot you down at first.

Telling someone they need to seek help is not always an easy task. It can feel invasive of their personal space. Being unsure of how they will react creates stress and possible conflict. However, if you're confident that they should seek help you should not shy away from the subject. Far too many people are lost each year to this illness because they don't seek help. We need to be more open as a society on the topic of mental illness and be willing to help those that are unable to help themselves.

When approaching someone about the idea of therapy, be open about the idea. Whatever your personal reasons are for helping them need to be put aside for the time being. This is about helping the person in question. Create a safe environment to discuss the topic. They may feel embarrassed or ashamed of how they feel and uncomfortable that someone else is aware of those feelings. Reassure them that it's okay and that you simply want them to feel better.

Try to use neutral unaccusing language when speaking to this person. What is happening is not their fault and making them feel worse about the situation will only drive them away. This is a delicate time where being calm and supportive will yield huge gains. Talk in a way that makes it appear as though you don't care about what choice they make. Seeking help is a personal decision and they must feel like they're the one who made the choice. Don't pressure them one way or the other and let them know you'll be supportive of whatever decision they make. I know you want them to get help but, thinking about the outcome we want can cause us to use words and body language counterproductive to our cause. Once the discussion is over all you can do is wait for their decision.

Be Patient:

Once you've talked to the person and made it aware you think they would benefit from seeing a therapist your job is done. As I mentioned before they may be resistant to the idea of therapy. This is okay and a normal reaction. One of the biggest hurdles to dealing with PDD and depression in general is the idea that one must want to get better in order to get better. They have to want to get better and seek help themselves. You have only opened the door for them. It may take a few days, weeks or months but, as long as you're supportive and talk about help in a positive way I am confident they will want to seek help eventually.

Everyone wants to be independent and it takes enormous courage to admit that we need help sometimes.

Finding a Therapist:

So you've talked to the person you would like to get help. Finding a therapist is a relatively straightforward process. The internet is a great place to start. therapists.psychologytoday.com/rms/ has an easy to use search engine that will locate registered therapists in and near your zip code. It has the usual assortment of filters and ways to sort results and every entry has a phone number listed.

Many therapists are also located in phone books and yellow pages. Some hospitals even have psychology programs with many different psychologists on staff. Finding a therapist is the easy part. Finding the right one is the difficult part.

Once you have located a therapist that is in your area and fits any insurance restrictions the patient may have it's time to give them a call. Offer to let the person in question call the therapist's office to make the appointment themselves. If they don't want to call be prepared

What does PDD Feel Like?

to make the call for them. If you are going to make an appointment for someone else I have to be quite clear about a few things. Some offices may not let you make an appointment for someone else. This is to cover themselves and make sure the patient is not being forced into treatment. This brings me to my next point. You can not force someone to go to therapy. It will not be helpful for them or yourself. Therapy is a highly personal thing and as I mentioned before the person in question must be ready and willing for change.

Before the first appointment it may be necessary to let the person seeking help know that if they don't like the therapist they are not obligated to keep seeing them. Therapy is a kind of partnership and it's important that there is good chemistry between a therapist and patient. If there is a good chemistry than congratulations. If not don't be alarmed. It may take a few sessions for the patient to decide if they like a therapist. If the patient ends up deciding they don't like their therapist it's time to find another one. Don't be surprised if it takes 5, 10, or 15 therapists until you find the right one. It will happen eventually.

If you need to be present for the first visit, here is a brief rundown as to what will probably happen (Every therapist has their own way of doing things.).

There will be forms to fill out. Some for you and some for the person getting help. Some will be medical and some will be about mental health history. After the paperwork is completed, the therapist will come out and either talk to you, if you're a parent or guardian, or they will simply ask the person in question to come back with them. The first few sessions are for the therapist to gather information on symptoms and how everything started. This will assist them in making a proper diagnosis and helping to design a treatment plan.

The early phases of seeing a therapist are an important time. I feel it is important to check up on the person getting help for the first month or so. They may think that therapy is dumb or not helping. Encourage them to keep going. Make comments on any positive changes you see in the person. As they continue to see a therapist they will slowly improve and should want to go on their own.

When they go to therapy because they see the benefit of it, you can finally relax. Many people never make it to this stage. You can feel good knowing you took part in helping them reach this point.

Helping someone with chronic depression can be tiring. Just the task of utilizing a therapist can be arduous. But, if after finding a therapist you would still like to help there are other things you can do as well. These strategies can also be used while waiting to find a therapist. They are simple things that detail some of the common and not so common hurdles someone with PDD may deal with. I have tried my best to verbalize things I wish others would have done for me at times. As always, everyone is different and what I suggest will not work for everyone. There are far more things you can try than what I have listed here. But, I decided to include two more things you can try while helping someone through depression.

Talking:

Talking with someone who is chronically depressed can be a great help. It doesn't have to be about anything in particular either. Oftentimes people with depression feel socially isolated and alone. Simple communication can go a long way towards helping them in that department.

I recommend you take on more of a listening role rather than a speaking one. Let them steer the conversation and simply go wherever they want to go. They may be a little hesitant at first because depressed people can feel like no one is interested in them or what they have to say. You may not understand everything they're trying to tell you and that's okay. It's okay to ask questions about what they're going through. There's a good chance they'll appreciate it. Most of the time people don't make an effort to understand how this illness feels. Having them explain certain things shows an interest to understand them.

It may also be important that you reach out to them from time to time. When you initiate the conversation it sends the message that you want to talk to them.

Talking is a simple and effective way to help someone through their illness. They may be negative at times and require many weeks of reassurance on certain things. Know that this is the illness talking and not them. It will be helpful to them to know that they don't have to go through this alone. So, if you're ever at a loss as to what to do, try talking.

Socializing:

Depression makes one pull back from social gatherings and being around people in general. The body feels sick and as such acts the way a person with a physical illness would. We instinctively isolate ourselves so as to not spread the disease. Unfortunately, in the case of depression this only makes things worse. So, this person will often times need a slight push to get them to socialize again.

Inviting them to events is a great way to help them feel included again. Depending on their level of anxiety they may need to start off with small gatherings first. So, make sure they are aware of what the event in question involves. Even if they used to be an outgoing person they may still need some time to readjust to a lot of people.

What does PDD Feel Like?

It's quite likely that the first couple of times you try to get them to come out and do something they will resist. This is a normal response. Gentle persuasion is the best course of action. Getting irritated or annoyed will only reinforce their belief that they should be alone. In some cases you may have to go to them. But given time, they will want to go out and see people again. They will realize they feel better even if it's only while they're out. Getting out and socializing does wonders for the depressed mind.

They will have good days where it's easy for them to go out. There will be bad days that it doesn't matter what you say and they will stay at home. It's all part of the learning and healing process. As long as you don't force them to do anything and reassure them that it's okay if they don't want to go out. Keep sending out the invitations and they will eventually accept. They need the help of friends and family to get through this. Not asking them to things even when you think you know the answer will only alienate them more.

Like so many other things relating to chronic depression time and patience will eventually yield positive results.

I hope this chapter has given you an idea of what depression is like and how you can help someone who is struggling with the illness. Having a strong support group is a key element in one's recovery. Just by being there and showing someone you care is a huge help.

I've tried to do my best in describing what this disease is like and laying out a plan to help someone get back to a better place. There will be times where the person you are trying to help may not seem like they're grateful. I want you to know that they are and sometimes it's difficult to show it. Chronic Depression is an illness years in the making and will likely take as much time to fully recover (if the person is able to fully recover). Even if they never fully beat the illness they will definitely be able to get to a place where their symptoms have a minimal impact on their lives. Working with someone who has chronic depression is a balancing act. One you will get more experience with over time. In the end the reward will be worth the effort and you will have a bond with that person like no other.

Chapter 3
Depression Physiology

After reading chapter one you now know that PDD has a variety of symptoms. These symptoms affect both the physical and mental functioning of the individual experiencing them. I think it is important to provide distinction between these symptoms and to show that PDD and depression in general is a physical illness as well as a mental one. There is an entire array of things going on in a body with depression. Learning about and understanding the systems affected can make treatment easier to understand.

In this chapter, I will briefly go over some of the physical characteristics of depression. This information isn't new or groundbreaking and is readily available on many different websites. I've simply compiled a basic understanding of depressive physiology so the information is all in one place. There is a wealth of in depth knowledge available, but it is outside the scope of this book. I wanted to give a rudimentary understanding of the illness so you have a basic idea of what is going on physiologically.

Overview:

As you may have figured out from your own research and/or intuition, depression is a multifaceted illness. It affects multiple parts of the body as well as the mind. Research has confirmed that this is the case and have documented that the brain of a depressed person is affected in several areas simultaneously. (3, 4)

While it has been noted that the entire brain is affected during depression there are a few areas that are more significant. These parts are all located within a system of the brain known as the limbic system.

The limbic system is an "old" part of the brain evolutionarily speaking and is sometimes referred to as the "emotional" brain. It's not hard to figure out why this is important to mood disorders. The limbic system is made up of four parts. Three of which are relevant to mood disorders. These three parts are:

Depression Physiology

- Hypothalamus

- Amygdala

- Hippocampus

These parts of the limbic system work in conjunction with other parts of the brain to allow us to feel emotion, our basic needs (hunger, thirst), fear and anxiety, and play a role in our memories. Next, I will give an overview for each of the three parts so you can have a better understanding of their role in the brain and how they relate to depression.

Hypothalamus:

The hypothalamus is a pea sized gland in the brain that sits above the pituitary gland and is attached by a small stalk. The hypothalamus is a complex part of the brain responsible for a variety of functions. The main function is that of homeostasis (the balance and regulation of a variety of systems) within the human body. It is also involved in functions such as emotion, thirst, hunger, circadian rhythms, and the control of the autonomic nervous system. The hypothalamus is significant to depression because it is also a key component in the stress response system of the brain. When a stressor is interpreted, the hypothalamus releases two hormones (CRH and Vasopressin) that eventually lead to cortisol being released into the blood stream (this is important and I'll explain more about cortisol later in the chapter).

Amygdala:

The amygdala is an almond shaped structure located deep within the brain. In order to keep terminology less complex, the amygdala is more or less located at the "bottom" of the brain. If you were to flip the brain upside down you would be able find it as a bulge hiding underneath a small layer of tissue.

The amygdala is involved in a variety of functions which are as follows: memory, emotion and fear. Relevant to depression the amygdala more or less takes environmental stimuli and decides how to interpret them i.e. what emotional response to illicit to said stimuli.

It has been shown that the amygdala is overactive in people with depression when shown something sad and under active when shown something happy or positive.

Also, being that the amygdala plays a large part in the fear response it is also involved in people who have anxiety as well. It's possible that this response is a leftover evolutionary trait designed for survival. If you are more sensitive to stressful stimuli your body would have been more likely to kick in the fight or flight response. However, this kind of response isn't as useful in current society and causes a variety of problems.

So, to quickly recap. When looking at a depressed individual, the hypothalamus plays a large role in the stress response and release of cortisol while the amygdala is in charge of interpreting stimuli and how we respond to them. Next up is the hippocampus.

Hippocampus:

The hippocampus is located under the cerebral cortex and has the shape of a curved tube. Humans have two, one on each side of the brain and it is responsible for long term memory and spatial awareness.

Unfortunately, as I am writing this there's not much information as to how the hippocampus is involved in depression. There is a lot of ongoing research right now about what exactly the hippocampus does in terms of mood. My personal suspicions are that the way we learn to encode memories can affect how we view past experiences. Coloring them in a positive or negative way. However, this is purely speculation, and I have nothing outside of anecdotal evidence to support this idea. So for now we will have to wait and see what researchers learn about this part of the brain in the next few years.

Neurotransmitters:

If you think of a section of the brain as a business, then neurotransmitters are similar to workers. Each has a place and a purpose within the brain and an imbalance of a certain type causes things to go wrong.

This is definitely the case with all types of mood disorders. For one reason or another the brain has a difficult time balancing certain types of neurotransmitters in the brains of people with mood disorders. This is not to say that this is the sole cause of depression, but it is definitely a contributing factor. While neurotransmitters are a contributing factor they may or may not be responsible for the onset of depressive symptoms. It's quite possible that a traumatic event alters brain chemistry (event based depression) or a person can be genetically predisposed to a less than ideal balance (chemistry based depression).

As a quick side note I think it is interesting that depressive symptoms can be caused by different things. It's even possible that how depression manifests is significant enough to affect how someone is treated. Scientists may find that depression caused by trauma is different from depression in which a neurotransmitter is out of balance. Research in this area is still in its infancy and we will have to wait for more studies to be published before this idea can proved correct or incorrect.

Now, I would like to cover the neurotransmitters that have been identified as key players in depression and mood disorders.

There are well over one hundred different types of neurotransmitters within the brain. Luckily, there are only a handful that play a part in depression. Better still, I'm only going to cover the three big ones that most people are familiar with. These are serotonin, norepinephrine, and dopamine.

Serotonin:

First up is serotonin which is, in my opinion, the most widely recognized neurotransmitter. Some people consider it to be a hormone (Which it can be. It is dependent on whether it is inside or outside the brain) but, this doesn't really change what it affects. As research and information improve this characteristic may become more relevant in drug therapy.

So, what does serotonin do? It is actually found outside of the brain and affects other parts of the body such as the central nervous system, GI tract, liver, and bones. So, in these instances it may be considered a hormone. When serotonin is used as a neurotransmitter it is thought to affect mood, social behavior, appetite, sleep, memory, sexual desire, and function.

When you begin to understand what processes serotonin controls, it's easy to see where depression related symptoms develop. A brain that is unable to properly utilize or create the correct amount of serotonin is bound to develop depression like symptoms. This is why we see certain medications target this particular neurotransmitter because it plays such a big role in the aforementioned areas.

I should also mention that while a decrease in serotonin is believed to be a contributing factor to depressive symptoms it is unclear as to whether the depressed state causes this drop in serotonin levels or if a drop in serotonin levels contributes to depression.

Norepinephrine:

Norepinephrine is a neurotransmitter sometimes referred to as a stress hormone. It is similar to adrenaline and affects the amygdala as well as the heart. Norepinephrine plays a role in the flight or fight response and triggers the release of glucose stores so our muscles have more energy to ward off whatever triggered the stress event. Knowing that the fight or flight response is controlled in part by this neurotransmitter makes sense when stress is brought into the picture. Another effect of the stress response going off is the release of cortisol which when elevated over time can lead to depression.

As far as mood disorders are concerned norepinephrine is still being studied. It is clear that this neurotransmitter has some effect on the brain but, it is unlikely to be the singular cause of depression. Symptoms of low norepinephrine include sedation, lower levels of alertness and (obviously) depression. On the other side, high levels of norepinephrine results in feelings of anxiety and high energy levels. As research continues on this neurotransmitter we will be able to pinpoint the relationship between norepinephrine and depression.

Dopamine:

The third neurotransmitter I'll be talking about is dopamine. Like the first two it is also a hormone/neurotransmitter depending on its location in the body. Its key role in the brain is to control the reward and pleasure centers. Dopamine is also a key part in "motivated behaviors". A deficiency or excess of dopamine is going to affect these particular systems and cause a variety of symptoms.

One of the more troublesome effects of dopamine is the role it plays in addiction. In drug addiction the substances involved can cause the brain to release dopamine many times over normal levels. This creates a powerful drive to continue to use that substance. Your brain feels as though it is being rewarded for using a substance that elicits this response. Other areas of the brain are affected as well. "The hippocampus lays down memories of this rapid sense of satisfaction, and the amygdala creates a conditioned response to certain stimuli."(5)

Because dopamine is involved with several areas of the limbic system it makes sense that it plays some kind of role in depression. Depressive symptoms such as reduced motivation, anhedonia, and psychomotor retardation are all linked to dopamine. While it is clear this neurotransmitter has some link to depression the why's and how's are still being discovered. The ongoing research about dopamine will hopefully shed some light on this powerful neurotransmitter and its exact relationship to depression.

As I mentioned previously the information here is a general overview of the three common neurotransmitters involved in depression. This is by no means meant to be a comprehensive or in depth discussion about neurotransmitters. I could write a whole book just on neurotransmitters and mood disorders. If you're interested in learning more there is a wealth of knowledge available online and in books.

It has become apparent to me while learning about brain chemistry that these hormones work as part of a system to create the complex moods and emotions humans experience. Unfortunately, our knowledge of these interactions is still in its infancy. As our knowledge of neurotransmitters becomes more sophisticated, we will learn exactly how they affect our bodies and find new ways to target and treat these imbalances.

Physical Stress Response:

Stress. It conjures up feelings of work deadlines, situations that make us feel anxious, and personal problems. Stress is usually associated with a negative connotation and as something that should be avoided at all costs. The reality is that stress is important and without it we would not have survived as a species. The stress response is powerful and alters our bodies in a number of ways.

While some stress is important to a healthy functioning body, just like most things in life, too much stress will cause damage. This is due to the complex nature of stress and how our bodies respond. For example, fatigue and muscle soreness can result from stress. While most people are aware of the physical implications of high stress levels, stress can also cause mental problems as well. In this section I will give a brief overview of the human stress response and how it is related to depression.

Firstly, I want to discuss the biological component of stress and what is actually going on when we are placed under stressful situations.

What is stress?

The Merriam-Webster definition of stress is "A physical, chemical, or emotional factor that causes bodily or mental tension and may be a factor in disease causation."(6) This is a good working definition and one that I think most people know. I would like to note the three causes listed here; physical, chemical, and emotional. These three categories can also be labeled as what are called stressors or things that evoke a stress response. I think most people are familiar with stressful situations.

We've all been stressed out by work, family, or other curve balls life can throw. Stress can also be caused by things we are doing physically and by foods or medications we ingest. This is why there are separate categories of stress causing factors.

Not only is stress caused by these three factors, stress also affects these three areas of the body as well. This is important because you will learn that stress is a whole body reaction. Almost every part of the body undergoes some kind of change during a stress event. Understanding that there are chemical, emotional, and physical responses paints a more complete picture of stress.

Physical:

Refers to things such as exercise or any physical activity that causes the stress response to begin. The stress response to physical stress is not always a bad thing. Exercise and physical activity initiates the stress response. However, this is often times a good form of stress (Eustress) and has positive effects on the body.

The negative side of the physical stress response would include things such as physical trauma, pain, or a rapid change in environment.

Chemical:

There are chemicals that when introduced into the body will induce the stress response regardless of how you feel, think, or act towards them. Stimulants such as caffeine and guarana will induce the stress response in the body. This is why these substances have energy boosting properties.

Emotional:

Yes, we can be the biggest factors in our own stress. How we respond to situations can induce the stress response in our bodies. But, not every situation is created equally. There are instances where a stress response is a natural and healthy reaction. Emotional trauma is all but impossible to handle in a way that will not illicit some kind of stress response. However, becoming worked up and angry over your coffee order getting messed up is something we can all learn to control.

Now that the three types of stress triggers have been explained I would like to discuss a general overview of the stress response. The stress response can also be called General Adaptive Syndrome and has three stages: the alarm stage, resistance stage, and exhaustion stage.

Alarm Stage:

This is the first stage of the human stress response system. When we encounter a stressor the body's flight or fight response kicks in and we go into physical overdrive. The body is flooded with adrenaline, noradrenaline and cortisol. These hormones are what allow us to perform incredible feats of strength and bravery when faced with such situations. While the alarm stage is useful in certain situations it does have its drawbacks.

Preparing for a stressful situation causes some damage to the body. Blood pressure spikes, blood vessels can be damaged, and tissue can tear. This is in addition to any damage caused by any actual physical activity. The body can only stay in this state for a short amount of time before the next stage starts to take effect.

Resistance Stage:

The resistance stage begins after the stressor has been eliminated or at least reduced in some capacity. The body begins to repair any damage caused during the alarm stage. This requires an enormous amount of energy, you will typically feel a little worn out and possibly even sore in certain areas.

While the body is working on repairing itself it is still on guard in case the stressor returns. This is particularly true when the stressor is persistent. Even though the body is continuing to try and fight its capacity to do so is diminished.

If the stressor persists long enough the body will move into what is known as the exhaustion stage.

Exhaustion Stage:

If the body has reached the exhaustion stage then it

has been stressed for a significant amount of time. The body's adaptive energies have been drained and this is where serious damage can occur. This leads to stress overload, burnout, depression, reduced ability to fight pathogens, and potentially tissue and organ damage.

As I mentioned before most stressors (at least in modern society) are of the psychological kind. Something happens or a particular thought or thoughts affects us in such a way that it causes our stress response to activate. For some of us, we have a hard time getting past our psychological stressor(s) which can lead to depression.

Understanding that stress affects the mind and body simultaneously is important to understanding depression. When we look at the symptoms of stress they clearly mirror those of depression. Because stress affects our mental and physical health so too does depression.

This makes it easier to understand that depression is not an isolated psychological or physiological condition. It is a mind/body illness. Realizing that prolonged stress is the key to depression is a huge step in understanding the illness as a whole.

To me this is one of the most exciting discoveries ever made about mood disorders. Learning it's not a case of "which came first?" made a lot of sense to me. I think once the idea of depression being a mind/body illness is accepted; it makes your treatment a lot easier. For me at least, understanding the illness goes a long way to making smart choices to further increase the success of my treatment. I hope it does the same for you.

We went over a lot in this chapter and by no means would I recommend you try to memorize this all in one sitting. Come back to it from time to time and if you want to know more you can use this book as a starting place. There is a huge amount of information on the biological side of depression out there and my brief overview of the topics I discussed barely does it any justice. So, I encourage all of you reading to learn more about depression and how it affects you physiologically.

Since I've covered the physical side of depression the next chapter will be about the mental aspects of depression. Things like negative thought patterns, the self-serving bias and habits (which will be covered mostly in chapter 5) are all discussed in chapter 4. While the biology of depression is interesting there is little we can actually do (outside of medication and exercise) to affect our body's chemistry.

The importance of learning about the psychological side of depression is that it will be a foundation for the things a depressed person can learn to control. Remember that stressors today are mostly psychological. Chapter 4 will go into what some of those stressor thought patterns are and should hopefully give you enough information to make sense out of the exercises later in the book.

Chapter 4
Depression Psychology

After reading about the physiological response of depression it becomes apparent that there is a lot going on in the body. It makes sense that we experience the physical symptoms of depression when our bodies feel like they are under constant attack. This is also true for our mental processing. How and what we think have an enormous impact on if we get depression and how long it lasts. This isn't to say that you can tell when depression is coming because it's difficult to notice; even for those who have had it before. If you have a traumatic experience, depression can happen overnight and would be difficult to stop. If it happens slowly over time, it's difficult to see the changes that happen because they happen gradually.

Depression Psychology

It's important to understand that our minds play a crucial role in the creation and healing of depression. Just as there are physical symptoms and responses to depression, there are mental ones as well. I will be covering the topics of rumination, motivation, negative thought patterns, the self-serving bias, and the mental symptoms of depression. While these are certainly not the only things affected by depression, I feel they are most useful to someone with PDD. Learning what they are, how to identify them, and how to change the behavior(s) associated with them will form a great foundation for your treatment.

The areas I will be discussing are ones that are the focus of a therapeutic technique called cognitive behavioral therapy. It's a type of therapy in which one learns to identify their unconscious thoughts and then slowly change them. I chose to focus on these types of behaviors because they are the ones that are the easiest to measure progress. There is an almost tangible effect that these processes of the mind have. Because of this, it is easier to see the positive changes you are making.

There are many other types of therapy and approaches to learning, understanding, and changing how we think about ourselves and the world. I would love to discuss those ideas as well. However, many of the other types mental faculties are quite difficult to analyze by yourself. They typically require some outside help, as well as, a significant amount of self-reflection. It is for these reasons I have left them out of this book. But, if you're curious, I have made some suggestions for further reading in Chapter 8.

Like Chapter 3 this is meant to be a brief overview on some of the things that can happen with the psychology of a depressed person. The topics I have picked are ones that I personally struggle with and ones that I feel are most common among depressed individuals. I doubt any of these things are unique to chronically depressed people but, I suppose how they manifest and the severity could be different depending on how long you have been dealing with depression. With that in mind, let's dive into some of the ways our mind can function when dealing with depression.

Motivation:

Motivation is the drive and desire to reach one's goals in life. These goals vary from something as simple as getting food to complex long term goals such as finishing college. Human motivation to accomplish anything is the driving force in life. Depression suppresses and inhibits the ability to follow this driving force. It fatigues one physically and drains the mind of the willpower necessary for achievement. Feelings of hopelessness can make it seem pointless to even try to start anything. This lack of motivation can be so strong in some people that they even have a hard time getting out of bed to feed themselves. While you may have one or many of these factors working against you, it is still possible to reverse their effects. There are many different steps you can take to lessen the effects of depression so that you can work on the things that matter to you.

On the days where you have little energy to give, it is important to do tasks that take very little energy to do. And to get started (you may have to force yourself) simply do something. Anything that gets you up and moving will be of great help. Having a pet or plant to take care of makes this a bit easier. Having another living thing depend on you for survival is a great motivator. For those of us who don't have that option, pick the smallest, simplest task you can think of and do that. Brushing your teeth, getting the newspaper, and taking out the trash. These are all examples of small things to do that will get you up and moving about. This motion is important. It is the movement that will give you the energy to keep going. Once you get going, don't stop. Sitting or lying down again will only put you back where you were before. There's a good possibility that you will feel uncomfortable and anxious most of the day. It's because you will be fighting the years of habits built up by the illness. Your body wants you to act a certain way when you feel depression the strongest. Fighting this feeling is not fun and it doesn't feel "right". But, it is an important step in coping with PDD.

Depression makes it difficult to finish tasks we start in a number of ways. Getting started may be difficult for some, and others may have a hard time working on anything for any length of time. These reactions to doing thoughtful work are perfectly normal. They take a bit of knowhow and understanding to work through. But, feel confident that the habits and road blocks can be broken so that you can accomplish your goals. I want to take a moment to clarify the types of tasks I'm talking about. The kinds of tasks that this work should be applied to are things that normally require some kind of focused effort.

The exercise(s) provided here and throughout the rest of the book are not meant to be used on everyday tasks or busywork. The exercises would work, but the effort required to do them properly shouldn't be wasted on small or menial tasks. Menial tasks may feel much larger than they actually are at first. But, this is not easy work and it may not be productive to spend the time doing exercises on tasks that take little time or that don't require much focused effort.

If you're like me, you have a terrible time trying to start things. This happens for a variety of reasons. There are other things on your mind, you get distracted easily, lack of energy, or you simply don't feel like doing the things you have planned out for the day. It's important to remember that this is the disease talking. You are not lazy, dumb, or unmotivated (in the sense that you don't have goals or desires). It is perfectly normal to have this kind of response to things when you are depressed. Many of the responses brought on by depression can turn into habit and all habits can be broken and changed. It just takes time.

So, how do we get started on a task? I assume most people just say "I am going to do this thing now" and get up to do whatever that may be. However, people with chronic depression have a few more obstacles to bypass before we can begin working on something.

I would like to share an exercise with you that has helped me in the past. It has helped me find alternative reasons for accomplishing tasks and the days I feel like doing much of anything is pointless. It will not be easy and will most certainly be work. So, I advise you to do this exercise (and any of the other exercises in this book) when you find yourself decent mood.

This kind of introspective work is difficult and may take time to get adjusted. Don't be upset with yourself if you are unable to finish this exercise or any others all in one sitting. There's nothing wrong with doing exercises in pieces. Do as much as you can at a time. Getting motivated can be one of the more challenging things you'll face. You'll still have days when you fight with yourself to get anything done. And it's okay to slip and not do whatever it is you had planned. As long as you keep trying. You can get there wherever that may be. Even if it's only a little bit at a time.

Core Beliefs:

The exercise I will be describing is one of the more helpful ones I've discovered. I admit it is probably one of the harder ones to implement because it requires a bit more energy and thought to accomplish. However, completion of this exercise will have a powerful effect and help you remember why you want to do the task in question.

We all have beliefs that make up our personality. These are the things that motivate us to be alive. Depression can bury those beliefs and make us forget why we choose to live. It is crucial that you give meaning to the things you're doing. Depression takes that meaning away and makes us feel that nothing is meaningful.

Before you can begin to improve your response to motivation you have to learn what motivates you. I mean really motivates you. These are the beliefs that make up the core of your being as a person. These beliefs are interwoven into your personality and help you make decisions. These are the beliefs you will turn to when you are feeling unable to do things or that the task at hand is insurmountable no matter how big or small.

Core Beliefs Exercise:

Take out a piece of paper and something to write with. At the top of the page write down the activity you wish to work on.

You are going to participate in an exercise known as "laddering". It is a cognitive behavioral theory technique that comes from the book Thoughts & Feelings: Taking Control of Your Moods and Your Life by Matthew McKay, Martha Davis, and Patrick Fanning.(7) It was presented to me as a way to help isolate core negative beliefs and work on changing them. You will be using it to identify core positive beliefs about yourself and use them as fuel to complete your activities.

Using this technique you will start with the activity and go through a series of logical steps until you find the core reason as to why you need to accomplish the activity. You will continue to ask yourself what each previous step means until you arrive at the belief fueling the desire to want to do the activity.

Example:

Activity: I want to exercise

What will happen if I exercise? I will lose weight and have more energy.

What will this mean? I will have energy to be a more present parent and spouse.

What will this mean? My family will know that I care about them.

What will this mean? I am a successful parent and partner.

You keep going until you reach a point where you can say "I am...". It is likely you will have greater or fewer rungs than the example. Whatever number you end up with is fine. Once you finish the exercise you will have at least one positive core belief about yourself. You can use this core belief to help motivate you on the days your depression causes the most problems.

When you're done put it somewhere in the open where you can see it. Or, if you live with other people and are shy about these kinds of things keep it somewhere close. Maybe in a wallet, purse, or even in the relevant task space so you can read it again when you're feeling unmotivated. Even if you don't fully believe what you wrote down, it's a start. As you continue to work on the why you will slowly rediscover what really matters to you and makes you feel alive.

This exercise isn't easy and it may take you several hours, days, or weeks to come up with an answer you feel is suitable. However long it takes is fine. Remember to try and do this when you are in a good place and I think you'll be pleased with the results.

Negative Thought Patterns:

Negative thought patterns may be the single biggest thing that happens when dealing with depression. This is especially true with people who are chronically depressed. I can tell you that my own thoughts suffer from this as well. All of the negative thinking, the assumptions about how others feel about me, and how I think others view me. These are all part of negative thought patterns. Unfortunately, "thinking positive" is not the answer. Our thought patterns are far more complex than that. While we can learn to change our negative thoughts into positive ones, it takes time and effort to make this change happen.

No one, as far as I'm aware of, has ever been born depressed. We are not born automatically having negative thoughts about a situation. This is a learned behavior. One that is shaped by our own personal experience, environment, and the relationships we have with other people.

But, what exactly are negative thought patterns? Well, let's say something goes wrong at work in your department. A depressed person will usually have a negative reaction to that. They may think "I did something wrong." This can lead to another negative thought such as "I'm dumb, I don't know why they ever hired me." This can continue for a while and usually by the end of it you feel pretty bad about yourself. This is one way negative thought patterns can occur. You have one negative thought and get locked into a negative train of thoughts all feeding off of each other. What's even worse is that often times we aren't even aware we've had such a thought. It has been so ingrained into our thinking that it happens without even trying.

This brings me to the next area of negative thought patters. Which is the emotional reaction to a negative thought. How we react to the thoughts we have is also a learned behavior. For instance, feelings of hopelessness and apathy are some of the common things depressed people feel. For many people with depression, even simple tasks can illicit these feelings. These are reactions that have been learned throughout our lives. How we react to a situation (mental or physical) is often the catalyst for negative thoughts and the result downward spiral. So to summarize:

1. You are faced with a stressor of some type.

2. You have some kind of reaction to said stressor.

3. Thoughts about the situation follow.

I must stress that even though these are learned behaviors and reactions it isn't your fault. Before depression you had no way of knowing what was happening. And, as I mentioned before, depression is a slow moving illness. It changes you little by little. Small changes are the ones that are most difficult to see until they've accumulated into something significant. In the following chapters I will provide some strategies and exercises you can use to change these behaviors. You will learn that these behaviors can be changed or replaced in a way similar to habits. On the following pages I have provided several exercises that will help you identify and learn to change your own negative thoughts.

Analyzing your thoughts Exercise:

This exercise and the one following are actually the basis of Cognitive Behavioral Therapy (CBT). If you're unfamiliar with CBT it is a method in which you learn to hone in and listen to your automatic thoughts. This allows you to identify thoughts that are causing you problems. Since depression, in general, comes partly from how we think this is a useful way to work on changing the habitual thought patterns discussed earlier. While the steps are simple, this exercise in practice can be difficult. The steps are as follows:

1. Notice a shift in mood.

2. Ask yourself "What was I just thinking?"

3. Write it down.

That's it. It looks simple on paper, but in actual practice this can be one of the more difficult exercises to apply effectively. Learning to listen to your thoughts is a skill. It requires patience and practice to receive the benefits of this exercise.

1. Notice a shift in mood:

Learning to hear your automatic thoughts is not easy. Most of us aren't even aware we have those kinds of thoughts. They are fleeting and often not even a part of our conscious awareness. So how do we identify thoughts we don't know we're having? We look at the footprints they leave behind.

Whenever we have a thought there is almost always an emotional attachment to that thought. While we can't always remember what we were thinking we can analyze the resulting emotional footprint. This is what noticing a shift in your mood means. As you go about your day pay attention to how you are feeling. Anytime you feel your mood beginning to slip take a moment and ask yourself "What was I just thinking?".

2. Ask yourself "What was I just thinking?"

Once you have noticed a shift in your mood take a few minutes and ask yourself "What was I just thinking?". Retrace your line of thought and attempt to identify what caused the shift in mood. Whatever thought this may be is the important one. This is the habitual thought or the beginning of a habitual thought pattern. It may also be helpful to take into consideration your surroundings and what was going on at the time your mood changed. Sometimes our thoughts are linked to our surroundings or certain situations. If you can identify a specific set of circumstances causing a specific thought it will make the next exercise a bit easier. Once you have identified the thought(s) responsible for the change in your mood record that thought.

3. Write it down.

Saving your thoughts is important so that you can start to identify any patterns in your thinking. This running log of your thoughts will help you analyze them more effectively. Reading a thought is much different than having the thought. When the thought is occurring it's difficult to separate all of the other factors contributing to that thought. By recording our thoughts we can look at them outside of our mind. This compartmentalizes the thought in a way. When we view our thoughts in a vacuum free from outside (or inside) influence, it's easier to transform or dismiss these problematic thoughts.

As you're writing down these thoughts write down the emotion attached to the thought. What you're feeling is as important as the thought itself. It will be important for some later exercises and it will help you reestablish potentially weakened emotional pathways. By learning to pay attention to how you're feeling you will be able to notice mood shifts (which will help you stop and lessen the effect of them) and you will also notice when something makes you feel better.

Give yourself at least a few days (a few weeks is better) to practice catching your mood changes. Once you've identified a few problem thoughts (or thought patterns) you can use the next exercise to create something more beneficial.

Transforming Your Thoughts Exercise:

Before you can begin this exercise you must have done the Analyzing Your Thoughts Exercise. You need to have a good handle on how you think and what kinds of thoughts you're having. Without that information this exercise won't do much for you. In this exercise you will take the negative thoughts you have been writing down and learn how to change them to something more useful. That way whenever you have the negative thought you can replace it with the more helpful one. Over time, the new thought will replace the negative thought.

Before you can replace old thoughts, you have to analyze the current ones you've identified. This is accomplished by asking a few simple questions.

How distressing is this thought?

This is the first question you should ask because it will dictate whether or not you spend the time and energy replacing a negative thought. You have to decide how much this thought is affecting you. How sad, mad, anxious etc..etc.. does this thought make you feel? You can rate your thoughts on a scale of 1-10 or percentages or anything you like. If you need some kind of visual indicator for the severity of thought then use one. The important thing is to have some kind of rating system that works for you.

Once you've identified the emotion evoked and the intensity, you can decide if this thought is one you wish to change. If you would like to change this thought then it is time to decide the validity of the thought.

Is this thought valid?

This is an important question to ask yourself when evaluating your thoughts. It is not meant to attack or prove your thoughts are unrealistic. It is a question designed to challenge your thoughts about your worldview. Our thoughts can be wholly true, have a little bit of truth, or be completely untrue (but we still believe them anyway). This question makes you stop and think about what the thought is actually saying.

A good example of this is when the words "always" and "never" are used. These are "all in" words and mean that whatever they are applied to happens (or doesn't happen) 100% of the time. I don't know about you, but there aren't a lot of things that happen 100% of the time. So, how likely is it that a thought you are having happens all of the time or never?

This is only one example, but there are many ways in which our brains trick us into having false thoughts. If you're having trouble deciding on the validity of a thought pretend that you're talking to someone else and they say to you the thought you are using. How would you respond to them? Talk to this thought like you would talk to another person. Once you've decided on the validity of the thought ask yourself:

What would I say to someone else who had this thought?

It's interesting how the shift in perspective can make thoughts that seem 100% true and overwhelming into something much more manageable. Seeing your negative thoughts in this way can also shed some light on how hurtful they can be. Many of the things we say to ourselves we would never say another person. Often times we damage ourselves more than anything else. It's important we remember to treat ourselves with the same amount of love and respect we treat other people.

As you begin to recognize the holes in your thinking it becomes easier to replace these negative thoughts. People only believe what they feel to be true. In doing this exercise you discover what is and is not true about your thinking. This makes it easier to change the faulty thoughts you have into something truthful, powerful, and helpful.

Once you've decided on the validity of your thought you have two options. You can create a replacement thought (untrue/hurtful thoughts) or you can accept the thought (true thoughts that may be hurtful or have negative impact).

Create a replacement thought:

This is where the real progress and change happens. Anytime you find yourself thinking the original thought you simply substitute it with the new more helpful one. Over time, you will stop having the old hurtful thought and should notice a positive shift in your mood. This isn't easy to do and will take time. So be patient and have confidence that with persistent effort the new thought will take hold.

It's important that when you're making this new thought that it is something you truly believe and stand behind. Don't create something that doesn't resonate with you. If you don't believe what you're thinking than it will be a waste of time. The new thought doesn't have to be happy and positive. It's more important that your new thought harmonizes with who you are as a person. As long as the new thought isn't causing harm it is a step in the right direction.

Once you have created and started to implement your new thought, don't be surprised if you feel uncomfortable at first. Similar to how exercise feels uncomfortable starting out, new thoughts will do the same thing. This is why it's crucial that your new thought is believable and true to yourself. The discomfort of changing your thought patterns will try to persuade you to stop and revert to your old way of thinking. Having a solid replacement thought will give you the confidence to ignore those feelings. In a few weeks those feelings will subside and the new thought will begin to feel more natural.

You can do this process multiple times for as many thoughts as you want. Focus on one thought at a time and eventually you'll find fewer and fewer thoughts that need changing.

Accepting your thoughts:

This is the other option when dealing with thoughts that are giving you trouble. You can either change them like I described above or you can accept them. Some thoughts are entirely valid. Even the ones that make us feel bad. Sometimes life works out that way and trying to change these thoughts wouldn't do anything for you.

As you're going through your thoughts you have to make a choice as to which ones need changing, which ones aren't that harmful, and which ones you can't change. If the thought is negative but not interfering with your mood then there's no point in acknowledging it. If it's causing you distress, but changing the thought won't do anything then you have to learn how to accept it as a truth. This isn't easy either because no one wants to feel sad or upset about things. However, sometimes there are things that life throws at us in which no amount of cognitive evaluation will help. Learning to come to terms with these types of thoughts is how you remove the stress that they cause.

How do we do this? There's not much of a process for it and everyone will vary quite a bit as to what works for them. I wish I could give you a set of steps that will ultimately lead to acceptance, but I'm afraid that nothing like that exists.

Acceptance isn't easy. It takes work, time, and a fair amount of effort on your part. Learning that a thought is valid yet depressing can be a big help. It means you're justified in how you feel. You don't have to feel bad about feeling bad. A valid troubling thought will make most people feel sad and down. It's a normal mood response. I understand that when you feel sad and upset most days it's frustrating. It becomes difficult to figure out which things are worth feeling sad about and which ones are not. Learning to accept certain thoughts helps with those feelings. It allows you to place your thoughts into different categories: ones deserving of a depressed mood and ones undeserving.

For example, I used to feel responsible for how other people felt. If their mood was bad or they were angry, I would somehow feel responsible. One day I had to tell myself that nine times out of ten I didn't do anything to that person. So their mood is not my responsibility. Once I accepted that idea and focused on incorporating it into my life I began to feel much better in those situations.

Of course this is only one small example, but you have to get a bit creative with accepting your thoughts and it might take some trial and error. But, like with anything else as you practice listening to your thoughts and working with them you'll find what works for you. As you discover new thoughts that require acceptance you'll slowly build up a skill set that allows you to deal with them as they come rather than letting them all build up.

Ruminating:

Ruminating is a word that many people are unfamiliar with. Even people with depression are unfamiliar with this word, though many of them do it all of the time. What exactly is ruminating? Ruminating is when a person has a thought that they go over repeatedly in their head. It is compulsive and typically focuses on one's distress. (8)

This sounds a lot like anxiety and general worrying but, the difference is that worry and anxiety focus on what could happen while ruminating focuses on past events. It is characterized by a lot of negative self-talk and intense criticism of the actions we took. All of this negative thinking and self-criticism creates a poor environment for positive mood and helpful thinking. The real kicker to all of this is that whenever someone ruminates they think it's helping them. They feel as though ruminating over something is going to make it go away or make them feel better about the problem. It's an interesting mental state and begs the question "Why do we ruminate if it isn't helpful?".

It feels like we can come to some kind of understanding or insight if we replay these negative events in our heads. I would say that this is probably the most common reason as to why people ruminate. Another reason is that some kind of trauma can cause rumination to occur. The type of trauma is not important, just that it has caused enough of a disturbance that the affected individual replays that event repeatedly in their minds. A third reason is that rumination is simply part of a personality trait. People with signs of neuroticism and narcissism are prone to rumination. However, this does not mean that they are unable to stop ruminating. Just like parts of depression, personality traits can be recognized and changed. So, if you happen to fall into this category don't lose hope. You can change your thinking habits. There are many exercises throughout the book to help with identification, changing, and implementation of thoughts.

Breaking the Rumination Cycle Exercise:

This exercise is designed to help you stop the endless cycle of thoughts that ruminating causes. It should allow you to break the negative thinking, calm yourself down, and allow you to focus your energy on moving past the thoughts or figuring out a way to deal with them in a more productive way. It's simple trick that works for me and one you can use too. All it takes is a little practice.

Whenever you find yourself stuck in a rumination cycle the key is finding a way to break said cycle (I know I know that's pretty obvious). The trick, is to do something that disrupts your thoughts so completely that your brain can't continue with them anymore. For some people this is as easy as yelling something along the lines of "Stop!" in your mind. For other people (myself included) they need to find something that completely absorbs their attention for a few minutes.

I've found that when I'm in a negative cycle of thoughts doing something that takes up all of my brainpower helps tremendously in getting out of that cycle. It doesn't matter what the activity is as long as it requires your full attention. Jigsaw puzzles, coloring, or drawing are good options. As long as it's something requires you to use your mind in an active way. Try to avoid things like reading, watching TV, or playing games. Those activities may allow your mind to wander and go back to the thought cycle you're trying to break. It will be horrible and not fun at first, but I promise that in a few minutes you'll feel a lot better.

Getting started is the hardest part when your thoughts are occupied with other things. Breaking the negative cycle will make you feel better and allow you to handle the thoughts giving you trouble in the first place.

Self-Serving Bias:

The self-serving bias is one of the more interesting aspects of human psychology. At least for me. It's something I was unaware of until I started to learn about habits and how they can color our perceptions of the world. The self-serving bias is part of our self-assessment. It's what we use when we evaluate ourselves on certain traits. Things like: How kind are you to other people? How hard of a worker are you compared to other people? How would your friends rate you on a scale of 1-10 as a friend?

These kinds of questions are designed to assess our place in the world. In our search for meaning and purpose, we will all inevitably compare ourselves to other people. This is where the self-serving bias plays a big role. Looking at this logically, most of the population is going to be average for these assessments. Some of us will objectively be above average and others below average. That's just the way things are spread out among any population. However, studies have shown that most people rate themselves as above average in every question and category.

While we know this objectively can't be true, it doesn't really matter to the individual as long as they believe what they are saying. If they believe that they are less lazy and more kind than most people they will probably feel pretty good about themselves. However, in depressed individuals it has been found that they are more realistic in their assessments. Rather, they don't have this self-serving bias that most people have.

This is obviously not to say that depressed people are not kind or lazy, but they know where they stand compared to most people better than those with a self-serving bias. This is fascinating to me. It makes sense that depressed people have some of the problems they report. They aren't constantly over estimating their abilities. I don't think this is a bad thing, but when we start to compare ourselves to what other people say and what we think other people are doing, it becomes a little clearer as to why depressed people can feel bad about themselves and have lower self-esteem. A depressed person is more realistic about who they are as an individual. When they hear other people talking about themselves (even if it's unrealistic), it can make a depressed person feel worse because they feel like they don't measure up.

It's an interesting idea to me and one that made my own depressive symptoms make more sense. It's interesting that by being realistic, we can actually hurt our self-image. However, it's not all bad news. Knowing this information could be a huge relief for some people. It can be liberating to know that how you see yourself is accurate and that's not something that a lot of people can do. It's not easy, but once you learn how to accept that fact I think it makes you a more genuine person. You aren't being fake. What you present to people is exactly who you are. Accurate and true. And that's something you can be proud of about yourself.

Self-esteem:

Self-esteem is a word that most people have heard of or used at some point in their lives. I think a majority of people associate good self-esteem with positive feelings about yourself and generally liking who you are as a person. Obviously, negative self-esteem would be the opposite of that. While these things are true, self-esteem actually goes a lot deeper. It has a lot to do with the core of who you are as a person. Self-esteem is part of self-talk (Which is something I learned from the book Self-Esteem Third Edition by Matthew McKay, PH.D and Patrick Fanning) and understanding how to have a good relationship with yourself.

Which brings me to one of the most important concepts about self-esteem and self-talk in general. Everyone has an inner voice, specifically one that criticizes you. This critical voice was named the pathological critic by psychologist Eugene Sagan.(9) This critical voice is the one that yells at you when you mess up, tells you you're not good enough, and discourages you from trying things. It's not a fun part of the psyche to handle. It's important to understand though because this inner critic and the idea of being in a relationship with yourself are tied together.

Perhaps I should back up and talk about self-relationships first.

I can't say if it's a cultural, societal or simply a human thing, but we tend to only think of relationships as being with other people. While this is true, we certainly have a relationship with ourselves as well. We are able to stop and evaluate our own actions. It's almost as if there are two people inhabiting our minds. This other part of us that evaluates our actions can either be positive or negative. It's important to remember that this voice is purely of our own doing. We are in control of what we say to ourselves even though it might not feel like it at times.

Now, think about how you talk to your family, friends, or a significant other. Think about the things you say to yourself. Would you talk to someone you care about the way you talk to yourself? I feel confident in saying no, you wouldn't. The negative self-talk and poor relationship we have with ourselves is often a strong component of depression and many other mental illnesses. However, remember that you are in control of this self-talk. This relationship with yourself. You deserve to be treated with love, respect, and understanding. Who is more capable than yourself to provide these things?

So, the pathological critic. It undermines your self-worth and fills your head with things that aren't true. It makes sense that you feel bad about yourself when you have a voice telling you things that would make anyone feel bad. Why does this happen? It's hard to say. Of course there are biological factors in play, but scientists still aren't sure why some people suffer from poor self-esteem. There are some theories involved with parental upbringing and others that say it is a defense mechanism designed to protect you. As most things involving mental illness everyone is different and it's most likely a combination of contributing factors.

The point being that self-esteem is a complex idea and is definitely outside the scope of this book. However, you can use the "Analyzing Your Thoughts" and "Transforming Your Thoughts" exercises to work on your self-esteem. Only this time you will be looking specifically for self-attacks. Anytime you find yourself attacking an idea, action, or feeling you have write it down. As you work on changing your thoughts about how you feel it's important to separate the attack from yourself.

Put the attack in its own space outside of yourself. Remember, if you wouldn't say it to another person why would you say it to yourself? Treat the attack as if someone else was telling you how they felt. How would you respond to someone you cared about negatively attacking their self-worth?

In closing, the complex interaction between self-relationship and self-criticism are important to combating chronic depression. These are things that will not change overnight and when you decide to work on them it will uncomfortable. The critic will fight you every step of the way. But, over time the critic will come to see things your way and you will be on your way to healthy self-talk.

Mistakes of Thinking:

I would like to briefly go over the styles of thinking someone with poor self-esteem or negative self-talk can have. They are categories of thoughts that are unhelpful or simply mistakes in thought. I think the biggest problem with these cognitive mistakes is that they feel so genuine to those who use them. Learning them slowly over time makes them feel natural and a part of who we are. Learning which one(s) you have will be helpful in combating your depressive thoughts. As I go over each of these I will give examples to help you understand and so that you can compare your own thoughts to figure out which styles you might be using.

These styles of thinking are taken from Cognitive Behavior Therapy, Second Edition: Basics and Beyond (10)

1. **All-or-nothing thinking:** (also called black-and-white, polarized, or dichotomous thinking): You view a situation in only two categories instead of on a continuum.

Example: "If I'm not a total success, I'm a failure."

2. **Catastrophizing (also called fortune-telling):** You predict the future negatively without considering other, more likely outcomes.

Example: "I'll be so upset, I won't be able to function at all."

3. **Disqualifying or discounting the positive:** You unreasonably tell yourself that positive experiences, deeds, or qualities do not count.

Example: "I did that project well, but that doesn't mean I'm competent; I just got lucky."

4. **Emotional reasoning:** You think something must be true because you "feel" (actually believe) it so strongly, ignoring or discounting evidence to the contrary.

Example: "I know I do a lot of things okay at work, but I still feel like I'm a failure."

5. **Labeling:** You put a fixed, global label on yourself or others without considering that the evidence might more reasonably lead to a less disastrous conclusion.

Example: "I'm a loser. He's no good."

6. **Magnification/Minimization:** When you evaluate yourself, another person, or a situation, you unreasonably magnify the negative and/or minimize the positive.

Example: "Getting a mediocre evaluation proves how inadequate I am.

Getting high marks doesn't mean I'm smart."

7. **Mental filter (also called selective abstraction):** You pay undue attention to one negative detail instead of seeing the whole picture.

Example: "Because I got one low rating on my evaluation [which also contained several high ratings] it means I'm doing a lousy job."

8. **Mind reading:** You believe you know what others are thinking, failing to consider other, more likely possibilities.

Example: "He thinks that I don't know the first thing about this project."

9. **Overgeneralization:** You make a sweeping negative conclusion that goes far beyond the current situation.

Example: "[Because I felt uncomfortable at the meeting] I don't have what it takes to make friends."

10. **Personalization:** You believe others are behaving negatively because of you, without considering more plausible explanations for their behavior.

Example: "The repairman was curt to me because I did something wrong."

11. **"Should" and "must" statements (also called imperatives):** You have a precise, fixed idea of how you or others should behave, and you overestimate how bad it is that these expectations are not met.

Example: "It's terrible that I made a mistake. I should always do my best."

12. **Tunnel vision:** You only see the negative aspects of a situation.

Example: "My son's teacher can't do anything right. He's critical and insensitive and lousy at teaching."

As you learn to listen to your own thoughts, these thinking styles will become more valuable. Being able to identify what you're doing enables you to plan ways in which to change how you respond to things. I think the most important thing to understand from these thinking styles is that they are all part of a negative thought process. While they may seem helpful, true, or positive, know that having these thoughts is not creating a better mood.

Most people do some of these from time to time. I know I still struggle with some myself. But, knowing about them makes it easier to catch myself when I begin to have certain thoughts. Because I know that they aren't true I can use that information to make sure they don't affect my mood in a negative way.

I understand that it can be a lot to take in all at once. This list is not meant to be memorized right away. As you begin to use the exercises in this chapter you can use this list to identify which cognitive mistakes you're making. With time, patience, and practice you will get better at seeing these thoughts in yourself and possibly even other people. It's a good skill to have and will definitely help you make more sense of why you feel the way you do about problem areas in your life.

Summary:

The psychological aspects of depression are varied and complex. However, it is integral to your treatment that you learn the basics. Learning about how we think and view ourselves in the world helps us to better understand our thoughts and actions. For example, understanding that depressed individuals typically see themselves in a realistic way helps to suppress feelings over underachievement. Learning how we come up with some of our thoughts and how to analyze them will be some of the most important skills you can learn. Because a large portion of your treatment will be done on your own it's important to have a solid skill set. It will help you from losing progress and allow you to cope.

I understand this is not easy information to process or even apply. I'm still learning about my own thoughts and how to apply this information to myself. But, it's a lifelong process and there's no rush to figure this all out in a few weeks. Consistent effort is the key here. Take things slow and work a little bit at time. You will be well on your way to more productive thinking and a better relationship with yourself.

Chapter 5
PDD and Habits: How to Identify and Change Them

Habits. They form the basis of our behaviors and how we manage to make it through the day without overloading our brains. They're the reason you take your shoes off in the same place when you get home and how you can drive to work and not remember the trip. We all require habits to function. However, just as we are able to create good habits, we can also create negative ones that affect us poorly. Which is part of the reason why exercise is difficult to start and cigarettes are near impossible to quit for some smokers.

PDD and Habits: How to Identify and Change Them

You might be asking "What do habits and depression have to do with each other?". First, we must establish what kind of depression we're discussing. While I feel habits are a part of all depressions, I believe them to be most prominent for those suffering from Persistent Depressive Disorder. It's really one of the only reasons I can think of that separates people who have a bout of depression from those people who get stuck in it for years. Out Of all the research and reading I've done, it seems to be that an individual's habits and habit forming ability are a significant determining factor in PDD.

Perhaps I should clarify. It is obviously not the only contributing factor because a person's genes, environment, current mental and physical state all play a role in depression. However, if you take all of those factors and make them equal, except for the habit forming ability of each person, I think you will find that they will have vastly different depressive experiences. It is for this reason, I have devoted a whole chapter to this idea and I believe it is crucial to understand this concept.

Learning how to change your habits could potentially be the missing piece to turning a person's depressive state around. Habits are powerful tools of the human brain. All of us can learn to use them to change how we think, feel, and function.

What are habits and how do they work?

I find that this is an interesting question to ask. Most people are familiar with the idea of a habit. They know habits exist and are somewhat important. We hear about changing them from bad to good. But, what exactly is a habit?

The more I thought about this, the harder it was to find a good working definition of a habit. To further compound things, I was interested in how long it would take a new habit to stick. After some research and a few books, I finally found my answer. It varies. This was dependent on several factors such as how complicated the task was, if you are trying to change an old habit, and even the person who is trying to change. There is a variety of things at work when we are trying to make and break habits.

But, first let me get back to the original question of what exactly is a habit? Well, it's difficult to give habits a singular definition. However, after numerous studies, habits are shown to have three basic characteristics.

1. We are almost completely unaware of them.

2. They are emotionless activities.

3. Habits are heavily influenced by context and environment. (11)

So for now we'll use a dictionary definition: An acquired behavior pattern regularly followed until it has become almost involuntary. (12) Using that definition plus the characteristics described earlier gives us a pretty good idea of what can be considered a habit.

Now, in order to better understand habits and how they affect us, let's examine each characteristic and what it means.

1. We are almost completely unaware of them:

This characteristic is more or less self-explanatory. What I'm talking about here is when we go on auto pilot. When you drive somewhere and don't really remember the trip, your daily routine when you wake up or get home, even how you greet family and friends. All of these things are habits. We don't think of them as such, but it's important to understand this because it has a significant impact on chronic depression.

While this state of unawareness seems like it would be a problem, it's actually a perfect way for the brain to conserve resources. Think about how mentally tired you are when you go somewhere or try something new. This is partly because you have to make decisions about everything when you're in a new situation. Without a neural pathway set up, your brain doesn't know how to handle the situation and requires conscious input. This uses up resources and will eventually wear you out. If we had to do this every day, it would be difficult to get things done. So, in order to circumvent this problem, the brain strengthens the pathways we use frequently in order to reduce the strain of decision making.

This is important to understand for chronic depression because thoughts can become habits as well. Just like with physical habits the brain will form pathways for thoughts too. What this means is that our brains can learn to respond with negative thoughts in certain situations. The more this occurs, the more susceptible we become to having a depressive episode. The good news is that all habits (even mental ones) can be changed.

2. Habits are Emotionless Activities:

Much like how habits go on auto pilot and fly under our cognitive radar so too do the emotional strains associated with a habit. If you think about it that makes sense. The more you do something, the more comfortable you become, and the less emotional flavor the activity creates. Driving, for instance, is exciting and new when you're first learning. But, the longer you drive the less exciting the activity becomes. Driving the same roads day in and day out becomes mundane and boring. However, go somewhere new and suddenly things become a bit more interesting. Sure, you might not be excited to drive, but there is at least more stress involved driving somewhere unfamiliar. While habits don't involve our emotions this doesn't mean that we are void of emotional response while performing a task.

Research has shown that the emotions you do feel while performing a habitual task aren't linked to the task at hand. Thoughts during habitual behavior usually have to do with wherever your mind is during said behavior. (13)

I think there is an important distinction to be made. When talking about depression and habits, the emotional response makes sense. At first it might seem like this is a case for how habits and depression can't really be linked, but I think it strengthens the case for that claim.

Simply because we aren't aware of the emotion attached to the task doesn't mean we aren't strengthening the pathways for that emotion. When the task was new there was an associated emotion with that task. Over time this emotional response dulls to the point that we aren't aware of it anymore. It allows us to think about other things and have emotional responses to those thoughts. However, if performing a habit increases neural activity for the habit I feel it also stands to reason that the original emotional response to the habit is also reinforced.

For instance if you feel responsible every time someone gets angry around you, that would make you feel bad about yourself. That feeling you get is an emotion that is now attached to that thought in that situation. Eventually, if you have that response every time that situation happens the thought (I am responsible for this person being upset) will become habitual. You would automatically think you were responsible for that person's anger. Also, the emotion that was originally associated with that thought will also be processed. As this thought becomes more habitual you will begin to notice it less and less. Likewise, the associated emotion will also be noticed less. But, even if you completely miss the thought and emotion your brain is still going to light up the same way. Even if you're doing and thinking something else at the time this event happens. This is why the thought exercises discussed in chapter 4 are important.

I also suspect that the lack of emotion associated with activities may play a part in feelings of anhedonia. In the beginning of a new depressive episode people often lose interest in things. Things that they used to enjoy. So not only is the habit itself downplaying any emotion associated with the action, the depression does as well.

Now we have a system that reinforces negative emotions and one that downplays and can create a lack of emotion as well. For these two reasons, I feel that habits downplaying the emotion we feel when activating physical and mental habitual behavior makes a strong case for habits and depression being closely linked.

3. Habits are heavily influenced by context and environment:

This basically means that habits are actions we typically do in certain situations. We all have our morning and bedtime routines. These are habits we have created based on the time of day and what we need to do. This characteristic of habits goes largely unnoticed because it's automatic. When everything is running smoothly, we hardly notice them. But, if something in the environment changes and we try to activate the relevant habit we notice them because the habit in question may not work. For example, on your way to work there may be a bridge. If the bridge is under construction you would have to find an alternate route to work. At first you may find yourself trying to use the same route to work even though you know the bridge is under construction. When our environment changes we have to remember to change our habitual patterns. These habit and context rules apply to depression as well.

You may have thoughts and reactions at work that you don't have at home for instance. Certain people may illicit negative responses out of you that otherwise you would never experience. Your environment could even be causing some of your depression. I struggled with feelings of worthlessness for a long time because I didn't have my own place. It made me feel like a failure at life because I had it in my mind that your own place was something successful people owned. I think it's important to take a few minutes to analyze your surroundings and the people in your life. If any of those things are a source of negative thought patterns and emotions, it's helpful to know what they are so you can work on changing or accepting them.

These characteristics of habits can be used to analyze depressive thoughts and behaviors. By learning about how you function in day to day life, you can learn to change the things you want in order to illicit a more beneficial mood. This kind of work is quite similar to CBT, but is looking at it from a slightly different perspective. Sometimes a shift in perspective is all we need in order to make sense of things.

Habits and Depression:

Now that you have learned what makes something a habit we can begin to explore how habits and depression can be linked.

One of the reasons depressed people can have difficulty doing particular tasks is due to habits. Habits can be good or bad. Brushing your teeth twice a day = good. Picking your nose = bad. We are forming habits all the time and a depressed mind still responds to habit forming stimuli. We receive and respond to stimuli a certain way. Except, in the case of a depressed brain, responses typically categorized as negative are the ones we choose to use. Being someone who is chronically depressed (or even in the middle of a depressive episode) you know how habits can stifle your progress.

As you learned in chapter 4 there are a variety of mental faculties in play when under the effects of depression. All of these things you can learn to control. Your thoughts, emotions, how you react to things, rumination, all of them. You have the power to change certain aspects of your mind. Just as you have the power to certain aspects of your body.

This isn't to say that this kind of work is easy. Changing habits in general is a difficult thing to do. We're used to interacting with a material world where we can see our changes in action. Mental changes are more difficult, in my opinion, because it's harder to see the changes as they occur and it can take weeks of dedicated practice in order to see results. But, just like any other skill, it takes practice and dedication to become proficient. Working on your mind is no different. I promise that if you put in the work you will see change.

I'm going over this idea in as much detail as possible because I think it is fundamentally important to changing how your mind works. As human beings we develop habitual thought patterns that dictate how we perceive the world around us. This doesn't mean that every thought you have is dictated by habit, but many thoughts are influenced by habitual behavior. Remember, habits free up your brain to focus on other things. So, when a habit is being performed you don't always realize you're engaging in said habit.

These thoughts can be brought on by almost anything. An event, a feeling, another thought, anything you interact with in some way or another can trigger these habitual thoughts. This thought process might look something like this:

Someone might be thinking about adding a deck to their house. They begin to look up the specifics of deck building. After an hour of searching they end up feeling frustrated and overwhelmed. They think "I'll never be able to do this." This leads to them feeling bad about themselves which in turn can lead to other bad thoughts etc... etc...

You see where I'm going with this? And we have these thoughts hundreds of times a day. Often times without even knowing about them. It's these thoughts that can trigger depressive mood states. So, our first task in learning to change these thought habits is figuring out how to identify when we have these automatic thoughts. The following sections will cover how to identify your habits and create strong plans in order to change them.

Once you have begun to identify your automatic thoughts and see when they are popping up in your mind it's time to start changing them. I realize there is a bit of overlap here and in Chapter 4. However, I feel the following two exercises are more suited for habits than the exercises presented for thoughts in Chapter 4.

Creating New Habits Part 1: Identify Habitual Thoughts

Building habits is rarely a simple task. Especially when your brain is fighting you every step of the way. Most of us understand that exercise and nutrition are important to leading healthy lives. But, the human brain has other plans for us most of the time. Our bodies are lazy and resistant to change. This isn't always a bad thing. It would be maddening if our bodies were able to change rapidly. Oftentimes it seems like it would be amazing to be able to lose that holiday weight in a few days. However, that would also mean we could gain it back just as quick. The positive changes we make in our lives take time which is a good thing. Pulling yourself out of depression will give you the skill set to identify the warning signs if you start to slip again. It makes it much easier to stop those negative changes and turn them around before they get out of control.

This awareness will spill over into other parts of your life as well. You will become in tune with how you think, act, and feel which will enable you to halt negative change in other parts of your life.

Habits can be broken up into two categories. There are habits that affect us physically and those that affect us mentally. I suppose an argument could be made that all habits affect us mentally since change begins with thought. But, I think for our purposes it is important to distinguish between habits that create a physical response versus habits they create a mental one. Mental habits will be the ones we're concerned about as they have the biggest impact on depression.

This may sound like you had some control over becoming depressed. Oftentimes habits are created without an awareness that they are happening. Many factors come into play when a habit is forming that it would be maddening to try and be aware of them at all times. Especially if you don't even know what you're looking for. There is some good news though. With practice and time you can learn to isolate the thought patterns contributing to your depression. Once this has happened it's possible to undo the damage they have caused.

Changing a habit is not an easy process. Our mind likes to fight this change which requires some creativity and planning to get around. However, with mindful effort habits can be changed.

PDD and Habits: How to Identify and Change Them

Depression can be looked at as a series of habitual thoughts that lead one to think a certain way and believe certain things about themselves. There are two major thought points relating to depression. One is self-appraisal and the other is the self-serving bias (which I'll briefly recap from chapter 4).

Appraisal is how we all try to find meaning in our world. It is how we make sense of things. Someone who isn't depressed obviously sees the world much differently than a depressed individual. Every time something happens to us, we are evaluating that event. The "how's" and "why's" rifle through our thoughts and how we respond to those questions has an impact on our mood.

The answer to why some of us can respond in a positive manner and others in a negative way is complicated. There are a huge number of life events and scenarios that can nudge us one way or the other. The important thing is how you feel and respond to said event. So, don't feel like this is somehow your fault you ended up this way. It's kind of hard to stop something you don't know is happening right?

The second part to explaining how habits and depression are related is called the self-serving bias. This refers to how someone relates to those around them. On average, people who are asked to rate themselves tend to do so at a higher level than those around them. In other words, they feel that they do better at things like work and school. They also tend to rate themselves higher on values such as charitability and kindness. Depressed people don't have this positive image buffer.

Before you can begin to change a habit you must first be able to isolate the problem thought. Even though this section will focus mostly on thoughts (where habits originate) these strategies can be applied to physical habits as well. So, how do we isolate unconscious thoughts? One way is through a thought technique called mindfulness.

Mindfulness:

Mindfulness is about learning to live in the moment and simply allow thoughts to come and go without judgment. It is about learning to increase your conscious awareness of what you are doing right now. As you practice this you will be able to recognize certain thoughts that are contributing to your depression.

Mindfulness is about learning to love oneself. You are being open and compassionate to whatever surfaces good or bad. It's not easy at first and definitely not for everyone. However, I highly recommend everyone try it at least for a little bit each day. Once you get good at it you'll be able to perceive your own thoughts whenever you want which can only help your treatment.

1. Relax the body and the mind

The first step is fairly simple. Do whatever makes you feel calm and at peace. Whenever you find yourself centered and calm find a quiet place to sit for a few minutes.

2. Concentrate on something

Most people like to concentrate on their breath but, it can really be anything. Just make sure you hold that object or idea in your mind as best you can. Your mind will undoubtedly begin to wander towards other things. This is to be expected and it is your job to sit and observe while working to gently bring yourself back to the center. The mental power required to concentrate on only one thing is quite difficult but, it will ease with time and practice.

3. Be Mindful

While the title is not especially helpful this means to simply observe your thoughts. Whatever surfaces look at it from the outside in as objective manner as possible. When the thought has passed, work on coming back to your focus until the next thought surfaces. Repeat for several minutes or until you feel mentally tired.

Once you become proficient with the practice of mindfulness you will be able to call on the skill in an instant. You will be able to observe whatever it is you're doing from an objective viewpoint. This will help you destroy irrational thoughts. The result of this is a better frame of mind and more energy to pursue your goals. You will be able to stop unproductive thoughts and emotions from squelching your mood.

Creating New Habits Part 2: Creation and Implementation of Change

Once you've become proficient at identifying any problem thoughts or habits you can begin the process of changing them. There are two exercises I would like to share that will help with this process. They will help you create a plan for change and give you something to work towards.

The problem with habitual behavior is that removing a habit is a lot more difficult than replacing one. If you've ever tried to change a pet's behavior you understand. These exercises will help you take the current habitual thoughts causing you problems and replacing them with something more helpful. These exercises are called the WOOP exercise (14) and Implementation Intention.

WOOP Exercise:

WOOP stands for Wish, Outcome, Obstacle, and Plan. This is a simple yet powerful exercise that will allow you to isolate a habit and create a plan for change.

Wish: Write down the habit you are going to change.

Outcome: Best scenario that will happen from changing the habit.

Obstacles: What will slow or stop the habit from changing.

Plan: Whenever the habitual behavior is activated what you will do in order to change said behavior. It is important to have specific cues that are easy to remember and have the right amount of specificity. The Implementation Intention Plan will cover this portion.

Implementation Intention Plan:

Implementation intention is a goal setting strategy. It focuses on creating If-Then statements to use as a means of behavior change. This strategy was introduced by Peter Gollwitzer in 1999.(15) Learning how to use this goal setting plan will go a long way towards helping you change negative thought patterns. It is easy to comprehend, simple to create a plan, and straight forward in its implementation. The If-Then statements of an Implementation Intention Plan are broken up into their subsequent parts when preparing to change a habit.

1. If:

The beginning of a good implementation intention is creating a situation that coincides with the habit you wish to change. It's important that this situation neither too vague nor too specific. Too vague and it will be hard to remember to do the habit in every applicable situation. If it's too specific, you might not get to practice the habit enough to illicit a change. Events that aren't focused around a specific time or a time of day are good places to start.

Let's say for instance I'm trying to incorporate more fruit into my diet and eliminate sugary junk food. A suitable If statement would be "If I get a craving for sugar". This statement doesn't use a time of day and it isn't something that is happening all of the time. I also know that I tend to crave sugar at certain times of day or after doing certain things like eating a bigger meal. A poor version of this If statement would be "If I eat a bigger meal" or "If I get a craving for sugar at night". The first statement doesn't take into account the problem and the second one is too specific and is linked to a time. If I were to get a craving for sugar at another time of day then this statement wouldn't work.

The real power of the If statement is to set up for the substitute behavior that follows. The "If" statement has to be constructed this way so the Then statement which follows will be able to do the job of changing the behavior in question.

2. Then

Obviously the second part an Implementation

PDD and Habits: How to Identify and Change Them

Intention Plan the "Then" statement is what drives behavior change within this goal setting strategy. Then statements are the action you will do to replace the habit you're changing. Then statements should be specific, something that is simple, and automated. You want this change to be easy to carry out so you are more likely to stick to not give up.

This is difficult enough for people without mood issues and doubly important for those of us who do. It is also advisable to give yourself two or three options for your Then statement. It can keep things from getting stale and gives lets you choose something else if you don't feel like doing your primary one for whatever reason.

Going back to my example from before: "If I get a craving for sugar, then I will have an apple, banana, or orange." My then statement is simple, direct, and gives me a few options so I don't get tired of one piece of fruit. I could also change the fruits every few days or weeks for extra variety. Now, this might not be a 100% ideal then statement because it might be difficult to always have access to the fruits I stated. The nice thing about a well written Then statement is that they are flexible. If I find myself in a situation without the fruits I listed I can look for another type of fruit to eat. Even better, if I know I will be somewhere without fruit I can always bring a piece or two from home.

This is not an easy thing to do. As I've said earlier and will continue to say, this did not happen to you overnight and you will not get rid of this overnight. As are most things in life it is a process. But, it is a process you can feel good about every time you make an attempt. Even if you don't quite understand the material or are having a hard time identifying and changing things at first, don't worry. There's not a time frame to get things done and there's certainly no wrong way to go about positive change. Everyone is different and as such will make their way through these exercises at different speeds. So, try to enjoy the process and know that you are doing some great work in taking control of your illness. This is all a part of learning who you are as an individual and you will come out of this a stronger person. All it takes is time, patience, and a little understanding.

To me, habits are one of the most important things to look at when discussing chronic depression. Habits could possibly one of the major components of how someone can become chronically depressed. When someone is faced with a stressful situation they respond a certain way. As we grow and learn, this response becomes ingrained into our way of thinking. Some of these responses are healthy and others are not. Entering into late teens and adulthood these stress response habits (if they are negative) can begin to affect our mood. It's this kind of habit progression that can cause someone to be affected with PDD.

PDD and Habits: How to Identify and Change Them

There are other ways it can happen too. If someone suffers a traumatic experience and the response is grief and a depressive episode, habits can lengthen and exacerbate the situation. What starts out as a depressive episode can become a chronic issue depending on what habits are formed during the depressive episode. I suspect that the ability at which someone can learn new habits plays a part in whether they are susceptible to chronic depression or not. If it takes you a while to acquire a new habit you would be less likely to change your thoughts during a depressive episode. If you pick up new habits quickly it's possible depressive thought patterns can be learned in a shorter amount of time leading to chronic depression.

The main thing to take away from this is that depression is the result of stress response over time. The amount of time and the severity of the stress required is dependent on the person. However, understanding habits and how they interact with your thoughts and actions may shed some light into depressive behaviors you may have. Since a large portion of who we are and what we do is determined by our habits, it's important to understand this part of human psychology. It will be incredibly helpful during your treatment to understand how habits work and what you can do to change them if you so desire. The want to change is important because when we're discussing ideas of personality and behavior there are only two options: You can either accept things as they are and work on coming to terms with them or you can change the things you don't like about yourself. Any other course of action is only going to lead to more problems.

In closing, understanding habits and how you can change them is a powerful tool at your disposal to help combat whatever problems you may be having. It is one I wish I had learned sooner in my exploration of chronic depression. I hope you find it as useful as I have and can take the necessary steps to move towards who you want to be.

Chapter 6
Clinical Treatment

Overview of Clinical Treatment:

For some reason whenever you mention clinical treatment to someone with mental illness it conjures up images of poorly run psych wards. I guess we can thank movies, TV, and the media for that. Hopefully, after going through what clinical treatment actually entails, it will curb some of the anxiety you may have about seeking help.

Getting professional help is one of the best things you can do for yourself if you suffer from PDD or any form of mental illness. Working with someone who has dealt with mental illness before is a huge benefit to you. You can get advice, closure, information, medication, and anything else you might need in order to heal and become the person you're supposed to be. Yes, there are some cases in which hospitalization is required. But, not everyone has to do that and in those cases it is always in the patients best interest to be monitored 24/7. People are put into partial programs and psych wards so that they can be in a more controlled environment that will hopefully be more conducive to their treatment.

However, if you're reading this text than it is highly unlikely you will have to face anything like that during your treatment. Unless you want to. You always have the option of admitting yourself to a program if you're afraid you may harm yourself. If you feel that way I encourage you to do just that. It is not a sign of weakness but a sign of courage to admit you need help. Taking the first step is the hardest.

The purpose of this chapter is to inform you of some of the common forms of treatment you can pursue. This is meant to inform, answer common questions, and lessen the fear and anxiety many people have when they begin to seek out treatment. Chapter 2 has a section on finding a therapist and you can use the same steps to locate any programs in your area. A therapist will also be well aware of the programs located near you and can help with the process of entering one should you so desire.

Therapy:

I should start by saying that a lot of people get psychologists and psychiatrists mixed up. The short answer is that most psychologists administer therapy and psychiatrists diagnose and can prescribe medication. Now, psychologists can diagnose unofficially and can come from a large variety of backgrounds. Psychiatrists will sometimes have therapy sessions with people but, it has been my experience (and this could be solely based on where I live because we have a shortage of psychiatrists) that psychiatrists almost exclusively diagnose conditions and help with medication management. So, you will most likely have both a psychologist and a psychiatrist. Obviously this will not be true in every case. But, I felt it would be useful to know that there is a difference and the capabilities of each.

Types of Mental Health Professionals:

There are a variety of mental health professionals in the health care system today. They provide a variety of services including therapy, prescribing medication, and social or peer support. These roles also may specialize in areas outside of mental illness such as marriage or relationship counseling. I will briefly cover the ones a depressed individual is most likely to encounter. There will be some overlap between most mental health professionals, but they all have varying levels of training and specializations.

Psychologist:

Psychologists are professionals with some kind of doctorate degree. They receive training in individual and group therapy. They are able to diagnose and treat patients with psychotherapy. They are required to log thousands of hours in a clinical setting before they are allowed to practice.

Psychiatrist:

These mental health professionals are medical doctors with a specialization in mental health. They are able to prescribe medication and also help with medication management. Psychiatrists can also diagnose patients. A few psychiatrists also perform psychotherapy.

Social Worker:

Social workers must have a master's degree in social work. They carry the LCSW (Licensed Counselor of Social Work) title if they are doing any kind of psychotherapy. They go through many hours of direct clinical study and are trained in individual therapy, group therapy, diagnosis, and case management.

Counselor:

Counselors a found in a variety of places with many different titles. The type and amount of training they receive varies from state to state. They are trained in diagnosis, group and individual therapy. Often times they have specializations such as drug and alcohol, marriage, relationship, professional, and family therapist.

A good therapist can be difficult to find. Its important you find one that you "click" with and understands your wants and needs. Not every therapist will be a good fit for everyone. It is perfectly acceptable to have a few sessions with someone and decide you want to try someone else. They want you to get better and would rather you find someone who you feel comfortable with than stay and not get anything out of the sessions.

Which brings me to another problem I hear from people who are reluctant to go to therapy. They believe that therapists are only there to collect a paycheck and don't actually care about their problems. As someone who talks to quite a few people about their problems, I can tell you that simply isn't true. Even though I'm not a therapist I feel confident in saying most of them feel the same way I do. They would not get into the profession if they didn't care about helping people. Therapy can be draining at times. It can be difficult to listen to people and find ways to help them with their problems. If a therapist truly doesn't love their work and is passionate, it becomes quite clear after a few sessions.

This is not a career you choose in order to make a lot of money. There are certainly much easier ways to do that. I understand many of you may be skeptical about therapy, but please believe me when I say that this is one of the most important things that you can do for yourself when seeking treatment. Remember, treating chronic depression is most likely going to take more than one approach. I encourage you to try as many things as possible to see what works for you. Don't get discouraged if it takes a few times to find someone that works for you. Most people who go through therapy have the same thing happen. I, myself, went through four or five therapists before I found one I really liked. I promise you will find a therapist that can help you with your problems.

Medication:

Medication. Everyone's favorite thing to talk about when dealing with mental illness. While I don't want to discount the importance of medication in treating chronic depression I don't want to make it seem like the end goal for treatment. New drugs are being researched all of the time and right now we have access to some of the best antidepressants ever created. However, not every drug will work for every person. There is a lot of trial and error involved and it can be quite a few months before you find a medication and proper dosage that works for you.

I know. That sucks. It's not a fun process and definitely one that can be quite taxing on you. It's worth it in the end though. If you choose to pursue a medication route know that you will find something that works and it will be worth it when that happens.

This doesn't mean you have to seek out medication, but I highly recommend that you do. It can be the crutch you need to get you to a place where you can do and see the things you want. I think this is an important idea when discussing medication. In most cases medication alone won't be able to rid you of your depressive symptoms. I tell people to look at medication as a tool. Something that allows you to get at the real issues. If medication helps you get out of bed and feel motivated enough to work on your problems then it's doing it's job. I think this is the real value of antidepressants. Their ability to lessen your symptoms so you can work on building habits and fixing your problems is invaluable.

I should also mention that all anti-depressants take a while to fully affect the individual using them. It can take up to 6 weeks before you notice any positive changes. This is one of the drawbacks of anti-depressants in general and one of the reasons why it can take so long to find a medication that works for you. Because they take so long to work it can be well over a year before you find the proper medication.

In order to help with the process of finding a medication I'm going to describe the major types of antidepressants and what exactly they do. As you've probably noticed by now I think that having information makes the process easier to handle and less terrifying. So, to get started there are four main types of antidepressants: SSRIs, Atypical Antidepressants, Tricyclic Antidepressants, and MAOIs.

SSRIs:

SSRI stands for Selective Serotonin Reuptake Inhibitor. They affect the neurotransmitter serotonin by blocking the brains ability to reabsorb it. Basically when serotonin is needed within the brain it hangs out in channels between the neurons. The SSRI will block the brains ability to reabsorb what has been released so the neurotransmitter has time to get to where it needs to go. This is a grossly oversimplified explanation, but is basically what's going on.

SSRI's are the most common type of anti-depressant prescribed due to the fact that they have the least adverse side effects. This is not to say that they don't have side effects and many people can have difficulty with this medication. Remember, prescribing anti-depressants still takes a bit of trial and error. What works for you may not work for someone else. That being said some of the side effects of SSRI''s include:

Nausea, Insomnia, Dizziness, Weight gain or loss, Tremors, Sweating, Anxiety and restlessness, Decreased sex drive, Drowsiness or fatigue, Dry mouth, Diarrhea or constipation, Headaches.

They are also more likely to cause irritation, hostility, and anxiety than other anti-depressants. You should also never stop taking them abruptly because the withdrawal symptoms can be rather unpleasant.

With all of that being said they are still the mildest of anti-depressants and most likely the first one you will try. (Depends on your symptoms and the doctor though.) Here are some of the common SSRI's you may encounter. (By brand name. Not actual drug name.)

Prozac, Luvox, Zoloft, Paxil, Lexapro and Celexa.

Atypical Antidepressants:

Some of the medications in this category have been around for a few years and some of them are fairly new. These medications function much in the same way that SSRI's do. However, they target different neurotransmitters either alone or in addition to serotonin. Depending on which atypical antidepressant you're talking about some of them have been referred to as SNRI's (Serotonin and Norepinephrine Reuptake Inhibitors).

As for side effects, there is more variety in this category and as such the side effects will vary between medications. There are some common ones that can be seen across all medications in this group and they are: nausea, fatigue, weight gain, sleepiness, nervousness, dry mouth, and blurred vision.

Some of the brand names for medications in this category are: Wellbutrin, Cymbalta, Effexor, Remeron, and Desyrel.

Tricyclic Antidepressants:

These are among the oldest of the antidepressants. They are referred to as tricyclic because they all affect three different neurotransmitters. They all block the reabsorption of serotonin and norepinephrine as well as partially blocking the reabsorption of dopamine.

Before our knowledge of the brain became more sophisticated it was easier to just target all three of the main neurotransmitters. However, this has the drawback of causing some of the most adverse side effects because they play with a larger part of brain chemistry. Also, because of this, they are often prescribed after SSRI's and atypical antidepressants have been prescribed.

There is the upside that tricyclics take less time to provide symptom relief than the other types mentioned so far. These types of antidepressants usually provide relief in about two weeks. Like other antidepressants these should not be stopped abruptly and have their own set of common side effects. These side effects include:

Weight gain, loss of sex drive, dizziness and nausea, dry mouth, blurred vision, constipation, difficulty urinating, sun sensitivity, increased heart rate, disorientation or confusion.

One should take extra interest in the heart side effects with this medication. Because these medications can affect your heart rhythm they should not be taken if you have a heart condition. So, make sure you talk to your doctor before starting any of the tricyclic antidepressants.

Brand names in this category of antidepressants are as follows: Elavil, Anafranil, Norpramin, Sinequan, Tofranil, Pamelor or Aventyl, Vivactil, Surmontil.

MAOIs:

The last group of antidepressants I will be talking about are MAOIs which stands for Monamine Oxidase Inhibitors. MAOIs work by reducing Monamine Oxidase levels in the brain. Monamine Oxidase is an enzyme that removes neurotransmitters from the brain. By reducing the amount of this enzyme in the brain it is believed to boost serotonin, norepinephrine, and dopamine levels. This in turn helps brain communication and is why they are effective in treating depressive symptoms.

These are the oldest antidepressants and a last resort as far as medication goes. These medications have a lot of complications because you have to watch what other medications and foods you consume if you're on one. They react with a chemical called tyramine which can result in dangerously high blood pressure. This in turn can lead to a stroke or heart attack.

Brand names in this class of antidepressants are: Nardil, Parnate, Marplan and Emsam.

Antidepressants are becoming more sophisticated and I think as we learn more about the biology and chemistry of the brain they will become more efficient. We are already seeing tests being developed and administered that can figure out the specifics of your brain chemistry. By pinpointing which neurotransmitters are out of balance doctors are better able to prescribe a medication that will give you the greatest chance of success. I look forward to the day a cheap and effective test will allow doctors to give someone a personalized treatment for their mental illness. I think that will be the pinnacle of mental health treatment and care. At least on the medical and biology side of things.

As a side note, there are some new testing methods claiming to be able to isolate your brain chemistry imbalances. However, to my knowledge, these tests have not been reviewed extensively so their accuracy is questionable. If neurotransmitter testing is something you're interested in I recommend you do some of your own research and talk to your doctor. You can decide for yourself if that kind of test is something you would like to pursue.

Depression Treatment Programs:

In addition to talk therapy and medication there are also longer term more intensive programs that you can use to help combat your depression. These programs can be a wonderful resource because a lot of times all you have to do is focus on getting better. That's also the downside to some of these. While in them, you may not be able to work or do other things. The focus is on your treatment and that can take up most of your time. That's not to say that every program is like that. There are some that would allow you to work as well as receive one on one treatment. It's really up to you and what you think you need.

Unlike medication these programs aren't really broken up into categories and will vary widely between locations. But, I've done a little research and will describe some of the more common ones that I've found so you can have some kind of idea as to what these programs will look like. Some of these take places in hospitals but, there are more programs now that have their own facilities specially equipped to deal with mental illness. As we continue to learn more about mental illness, I believe more facilities like this will continue to come up.

Partial Programs:

Partial programs may be the most common type of mental illness program that you encounter. At least it was the one I was most familiar with before writing this book. They are also known as PHP (Partial Hospitalization Program) programs. The defining characteristic of these types of programs is that the patient continues to live at home, but has to commute to the treatment center up to seven days a week.

The type of treatment you receive will vary between locations. They may include things like one on one therapy, group therapy, medication management, life skills, coping skills, and help with substance abuse. The biggest benefit of partial programs is that you are still able to work and take care of your family if that is a concern. Because you are not required to stay at the center itself. This allows you a little more freedom in how you go about your treatment.

Inpatient Treatment Centers:

These are the types of programs where you go and spend all of your time at the facility. These can be broken up into two categories. Residential and non-residential inpatient.

Non-residential inpatient would be hospital and psych ward locations. They take place in a medical building and (I can't say for certain) you may be placed with people of varying levels of psychiatric illness. While you may have mild to severe chronic depression you could be living with people who have schizophrenia, bipolar disorder, PTSD or any other variety of illness. I realize that this may seem a little scary or undesirable, but there are many fantastic programs that take place in hospitals.

Residential inpatient facilities feel more like living at home. The environments are more comfortable and you will be placed with people who have similar mood disorders. This can help with a sense of belonging. It can be helpful to have other people to talk to who are going through the same things you are going through. These locations provide the same type of treatment you would get in a psychiatric hospital, just in a more comfortable setting.

There is another type of inpatient program called luxury depression disorder facilities. These are like residential programs except these locations are more like resorts. They feature beautiful scenery and modern facilities. The downsides to these is that they will cost more than a regular inpatient program and you will most likely have to travel some distance for one.

The biggest benefit to these types of programs is that you can work on your illness on your own time. There are no pressures from the outside world to get better. You don't' have to worry about work, family, or any of the other responsibilities you may have. This can also be a drawback if you're unable to be away from family or your job. However, do not discredit the effectiveness of having little responsibilities. Chronic depression takes an enormous amount of mental and physical resources. Lessening the mental and physical load you experience everyday could be the boost you need to significantly recover.

Clinical care is one of the best ways that you can combat your depression. Working with trained professionals will give you the best chance of lessening or removing your depression entirely. For most people a combination of therapy and medication will be sufficient. But, there are more intense programs for people who think they need or want more help. If you decide to pursue this course of action, check out the resources chapter for phone numbers and websites you can use to learn what is available in your area. I know that seeking professional help can be scary and you will have a lot of questions. I've tried my best to give a decent overview of what you can expect. Do your own research and talk to people in the field to get a good idea of what will work best for you. Remember, this is a highly personal journey and you have to do what will work best for you.

Chapter 7
Coping and Self-Care

In the last chapter I outlined the different kinds of professional care that you can undergo to treat PDD. These types of programs work wonderfully for some people and hardly at all for others. This is one of the reasons that PDD (and mental illness in general) can be difficult to treat. Everyone is different and your treatment should be tailored to your specific situation. Oftentimes more than one type of treatment needs to be administered at the same time to achieve the desired result. This is most commonly seen when a patient is on medication and undergoing some kind of therapy.

However, clinical drugs and therapy are not the only ways that you can battle PDD. There are many other things you can change in your life to make the illness more manageable and possibly even rid yourself of it for good. These changes are essentially the opposite of what the illness and your brain are telling you to do. As I explained in previous chapters, depression is partially the result of habit and it is possible to change and reverse these habits. This kind of cognitive therapy typically requires professional help to be successful. However, I understand that therapy is not always an option for everyone. So, in this chapter I wanted you to be aware of other forms of treatment that you can do on your own or in conjunction with professional care. I cannot promise that these alternative suggestions will cure your depression. I do however, feel confident in saying that using several of these will help to lessen your symptoms. This in turn will make your professional treatment easier and more effective along with allowing you the possibility of more successful self-care.

I have split self-care strategies into two categories. Physical self-care and mental self-care. The physical section will explore things you can do with your body to help with chronic depression symptoms. The mental section will discuss ways to affect your thought processes to accomplish the same goal. I do not believe that one is more important than the other in fighting chronic depression. However, I do feel that the physical strategies are easier to implement than the mental ones. Controlling one's body is something we are accustomed to doing every day. Learning to control our thoughts, which seem to come from nowhere, is a bit more difficult.

When beginning to add these habits and practices to your daily routine, remember to go slow and add one thing at a time. Use the habit building exercises from Chapter 5 to slowly add these into your routine. Feel free to add as many or as few of them as you like. It is likely that not all of these will be effective for you. We are all individuals and what works for one of us will not work for everyone. So, don't get discouraged if something doesn't seem to be working. It's a step in learning what works best for you. Keep on pressing forward and you will find the things that help you the most. Now, without further delay, let's jump into the section on physical strategies.

Physical

Sunshine:

Humans need sunlight for various reasons. This is doubly true for people suffering from any type of depression. I would even go as far as saying it's more important for anyone suffering from PDD. This is due to the chronic nature of the illness. For a standard depressive episode, getting more sunlight will boost your mood and potentially jump start your recovery process. Someone with PDD needs to make consistent effort to get enough sunlight to reverse the habits built up. It's not always easy and can be pretty difficult certain times of the year. But, I feel that it is one of the easier things you can do. The amount of time spent versus the benefit is quite large.

Some studies suggest that serotonin levels are boosted when exposed to adequate sunlight (16) As you learned in chapter 4, serotonin is one of the three important neurotransmitters shown to have an effect on mood. Sunlight also helps us regulate our circadian rhythms which can help with the sleep issues depression can (and oftentimes does) cause.

As little as 15-30 min of direct sunlight a day is all that you need to benefit from its mood boosting properties. If you are unable to get outside or it is a time of the year when there is less sunlight light boxes are also a fine alternative. A light box is essentially a bright light. It has specially made bulbs that produce much more light than standard house lighting. They are great for helping you reset your biological clock since you can "prescribe"" when to use them. If you wish to use a light box, I recommend getting one with a rating of at least 10,000 lux for white light.

Exercise:

Exercise is one of the best ways to help manage your mood.

Coping and Self-Care

This is especially true in people with chronic depression. It gets the body moving which counteracts the stagnant feelings associated with the illness. The body releases many different hormones during and after exercise which will help to elevate your mood. Your body will go through some positive physical changes which I will lead to a better self-image and more self-confidence. These are only the benefits in relation to PDD. I haven't even talked about the regular benefits of exercise that you'll also experience. There is a lot of literature on the normal health benefits of exercise and is outside the scope of this book to cover. However, there is a section at the end of the book with additional reading material if you desire to acquire more information.

Now, to get into the numbers part of exercise. How much? How often? How long? I could give you the recommended numbers for a typical exercise program. However, you will have a different goal with your exercise. The exercise program you undertake will be geared towards lifting your mood and creating a lifelong habit. So, for right now the amount of exercise you should be doing is whatever makes you feel better. Any activity is fine as long as it gets you outside in the sun (weather permitting) and sufficiently stresses your body into releasing endorphins.

When you're starting out you probably won't need to exercise for long. It's okay, you're not training for a competition (yet). Remember, you're creating a habit that you can build upon later and it's best to not overwhelm yourself at first. So, doing whatever activity you choose until sufficient stress has been achieved is the goal. Exercise is a type of stress called eustress which your body processes as a good thing. It actually resembles something more like excitement and is what causes your body to release endorphins. These are the feel good hormones that are released to help combat stress and pain. It is at this point you have been sufficiently stressed to feel mood lifting benefits of exercise.

You should be doing this activity on most days (5-7 days a week). I say most days because I know that you will have bad days when it will be incredibly difficult to motivate yourself to exercise. It's okay when this happens, change takes time and it also takes the same amount of time to undo the changes you've created. But, planning out the time in advance helps to keep the habit alive until you get to a point where you won't feel right if you don't get your exercise in for the day.

The kind of exercise you do is entirely up to you. I recommend some kind of cardio since it gets the whole body moving and will most likely push you to your stress threshold faster than lifting will. But, if you really hate cardio, lifting weights or some kind of strength training is fine as well. Just make sure you do a little something outside to get sunlight exposure. A nice walk or hike are two easy solutions. The other reason I suggest starting with some kind of cardio is that exercising that way is less complicated than setting up a strength program. And since you may be coming from a place where you have a hard time doing simple tasks it's important to make things as simple as possible in the beginning.

So remember, the key points to setting up your exercise program right now are:

1. Find the time and intensity it takes to sufficiently stress your body

2. Be as consistent as possible

3. Keep things simple!

If you can follow these three points you will be exercising more frequently and should notice a change in your overall mood within a few weeks.

Normally, if I was creating an exercise program for someone, I would evaluate their starting point and design a program specifically for them. Since I obviously can't be there to evaluate your starting point I had to attempt and create specific yet flexible guidelines you can implement in your own life. I know that it can feel a little overwhelming, especially with everything else you may have going on in your life. But, this coping strategy is less about traditional exercise and more about movement.

Chronic Depression: A User's Manual

There are days when I wake up and all I want to do is lay in bed or sit in front of the computer bouncing between the same three sites all day. These kinds of days are when moving is the most important. It's easy to sit and marathon a TV show or video game. Oftentimes these media outlets offer a distraction from ourselves and gives relief to the mental torment chronically depressed people put themselves through. These are the days when getting up and moving around will provide the energy boost needed to accomplish tasks. It doesn't have to be anything strenuous either. Doing anything other than sitting will make the lazy days easier. If you can get outside to add sunshine into the equation the effects are even greater.

I prefer a short walk or a hike if I'm feeling sluggish. Yoga, dancing, or playing with a pet for ten or fifteen minutes works just as well. Whatever it is as long as it gets your heart rate up a little and takes your mind off of the big bad task at hand, it's working. Then, whenever you feel ready, you simply come back inside or go to wherever it is you must be in order to work and begin. Don't worry about anything else on your way there. Don't stop for food, don't stop to use the computer, don't stop for anything (short of a real emergency). You worked hard to give yourself the gift of usable energy. Don't waste that gift on the things that can wait.

Diet:

What we eat plays a huge role in what happens to our bodies. Many diseases are caused by poor diets and I could probably write an entire book on proper diet alone. The processed garbage we put into our bodies day after day has an adverse effect on our physical as well as mental health. Most people know there is an obesity epidemic in the country now. Obesity is a physical effect that is easy to observe and one that we know is linked to what we eat and how much we exercise. I feel confident in saying that most people don't know that our diets can affect our mental health as well. Diets high in processed foods, meats, and fats make us more susceptible to depressive symptoms. The obvious answer to this problem is to simply observe a healthful diet in one's life. I realize that this is easier said than done because food habits are some of the hardest for people to break.

Food addictions are a very real thing. While we may not experience withdrawal symptoms or adverse effects like with drugs, it is important to know that people with poor diets have a food addiction of some kind. Some people are addicted to sugar, salt, or greasy fast foods. The human brain is partly to blame for these addictions. It is a leftover trait from having to survive in the wilderness where foods with these flavors were scarce. We needed to get as much of them as we could when we found them. The body needed them to survive and in response to that our brains caused us to crave and seek out foods that fit these flavor profiles.

Now we can go to the store or local restaurant to have these cravings met. The processed foods are so loaded with salt, sugar, and fat that eating real food doesn't satisfy the craving for these flavors. The density of these nutrients in processed foods is so great that real food is unappealing for many people. However, there is hope. It is entirely possible to kick these cravings and give your body the nutrition it deserves, which in turn, will drastically improve your mental and physical well-being.

A proper guide to nutrition would be a book in and of itself. There are some suggestions to find more nutrition information in the resources chapter. However, I can suggest a few simple things that should get you moving in the right direction.

1. Less Meat and more Fruits and Vegetables

I know, I know. This is a big one for a lot of people. I'm not saying you have to cut meat out of your diet entirely (although you are certainly welcome to do that). You only have to reduce the amount you consume. Instead of making meat the main portion of the dish, treat it as a side. Substitute dark green leafy vegetables instead. Variety is important. It's crucial for micro-nutrition and will help keep things from getting repetitive. This also doesn't have to be a change overnight. Change your diet a little at a time and you will be less likely to revert back to your old diet.

2. Reduce the Amount of Processed Foods You Consume

There have been studies done that show processed sugars and simple carbohydrates when over consumed can make us more susceptible to depression. (17) This doesn't conclusively show that diets high in carbohydrates will lead to depression. It only suggests that a link is possible. This kind of diet may create an environment (biochemically) that makes someone more susceptible to depression. It could also mean that people with depression simply crave more carbohydrate rich foods. It's bit of a "chicken or the egg" problem.

However, reducing the amount of processed foods you eat has other benefits. Even though there isn't conclusive evidence between diet and mental health, taking care of your body will allow you to handle the illness more effectively. For instance, fatigue could be a sign of diet problem and not one of your depressive symptoms. It could also be compounding any depressive fatigue you may have. If you can reduce or eliminate fatigue it would give you more energy to tackle other problems caused by depression. Remember, proper treatment of depression will most likely require changes on multiple fronts.

3. Reduce Consumption of Alcohol and Nicotine

Depression causes pain. Pain is uncomfortable. No one wants to be in pain for a few minutes let alone for days at a time. Unfortunately, for people with depression, this is the case. Why does this happen? Because there is evidence that suggests emotional pain is as real as physical pain. The "areas that support the sensory components of physical pain (secondary somatosensory cortex; dorsal posterior insula) become active."(18)

Even if you're not dealing with mental illness I would advise against using these substances. But, for someone with depression alcohol and nicotine cannot only exacerbate your symptoms, they can become a coping mechanism. This is undesirable because you will end up consuming more of these harmful substances and it will halt or reverse any progress you have made.

Using them as a coping mechanism essentially distracts you from whatever the real issues are. The addiction that can form from excessive consumption of alcohol and nicotine covers up what is causing you so much pain and discomfort. You won't be able to get better until you welcome that discomfort and learn to accept or change it.

4. Avoid all forms of illegal drugs

These should be avoided for the same reasons as nicotine and alcohol. In addition to those reasons, illegal substances can land you in prison and cause irreparable damage to your body. I know. It's easier to mask the pain of depression with some other substance or activity. I used to do the same thing when I would play video games for extended periods of time. Depression sucks. It hurts. It's uncomfortable. It isn't fun. But, using something to cover all of that up doesn't help you. If you truly want to get better you must have the courage to face that pain.

Social Interaction:

Humans are social creatures. We crave attention and social belonging in our lives. Even the most introverted of us still need some interaction with another person from time to time. We all have different social needs whether that be seeing people one hour a day or ten. You know what you need so don't feel as though you have to take every invitation you receive. That's not the point of socializing. But, don't decline every invitation either. Social isolation tends to affect most people's mood in a negative way.

This can be one of the harder things to manage with depression (at least for me it was and still is to some degree). Depression can be quite isolating and can make us think that people don't care about us. The lack of energy makes interacting with strangers as well as friends and family exhausting. However, the upside is that making the effort to see people has some strong positive effects on mood.

Depending on how long you've been dealing with depression, the amount of social opportunity for you could be quite low. Mood disorders can wind up pushing people away and make it difficult for family to relate to how we're feeling. This can make social interaction of any kind difficult. Especially if you have social anxiety on top of everything else. However, you can improve this area of your life and even significantly reduce any anxiety you may have about interacting with people. It only takes practice, patience, and a bit of courage. Below I've outlined some strategies you can implement to help. Even if you don't care for any of these ideas I hope they at least spur some creative thought that allows you to come up with something that does work for you.

Friends and Family:

Close friends and family are a great place to start when trying to introduce more social activity into your life. They are people you know and most likely feel comfortable around. They can act as a kind of anchor when you go to social gatherings. Having someone you know in a new place or meeting new people can be a huge relief.

Coping and Self-Care

Even if you haven't spoken to friends or family recently, open up that line of communication again. They will be glad to hear from you. Any doubts you have, remember that poor self-esteem can make us project our insecurities on other people. We can't know what other people think without asking them.

If depression is a new diagnosis for you explain to your friends and family that you might not always feel like doing things with them. Depression does that and it's fine to say no on days you're having a tough time or want to be alone. Make it clear that if you decline an invitation to not take it personally and ask again another day. Getting back into a regular social schedule takes a lot of trust and communication. The earlier you open that line of communication the easier it will be to establish.

Online:

There are a multitude of forums online dedicated to mood disorders of all types. These are great places to become part of an active community and interact with other people. The nice thing about online interaction is that it removes almost all of the social anxiety that can come from being in public. I caution you about using a forum as your sole form of social interaction though. While it may allow you some form of human contact it's important to interact with people in public as well. With that being said, I still think forums are a great tool. They can be used as a stepping stone towards in person interaction.

Online games can also be a valid form of social interaction. Especially if you have a headset and are able to communicate with other players via voice chat. Real time verbal communication is something I find to be quite helpful on days I'm not able to get out and see someone in person. Talking via a game or Skype is almost as good.

A word of caution with games though. I would not pick anything that has a competitive aspect. Stick to games or modes that are cooperative in nature in order to reduce the risk of finding toxic players. As a fairly avid gamer, I find competitive games to have the highest number of negative players. The win/loss mechanic makes people a little emotional at times. Similar to how people react during sports. Games without clear victory conditions and low penalties for mistakes are good candidates.

With all of that being said, the internet is a great tool for social interaction. There are far more ways to use the internet for this purpose other than those I have listed. I've personally used the ones I've talked about and have found them to be helpful. Find what works for you, what you're comfortable with, and don't be afraid to push yourself a little bit.

Social Clubs:

If you feel up to it, joining a club of some kind can be a great way to meet new people and become socially comfortable. If you're in high school or college there are many different clubs and activities to join. Find one that shares an interest you have and go to a few meetings. If you can't find one, then speak to the proper individual(s) to create a club. You might be surprised by who shows up.

If you're not in school there are sites to find social clubs and meet ups in your area. There's also the option of taking classes, courses, and workshops to find people who share a common interest.

I'm mentioning shared interests so much because it can be comforting to know that you'll have something to talk about. Being around people who like the same things as you means they're more likely to understand you on a deeper level. These are all things that make social interaction important for humans. The sense of belonging you can get from people who understand you makes a difference.

These are some of the things a person with depression can work on that affect them physically. All of the things I've just talked about affect your body in one way or another. In the next section I will discuss some of the strategies you can do that will affect your mental state.

While the mind and body are connected, coping strategies tend to affect one system and then the other. Physical changes in mood will help create a better state of mind and working on things thought of as "mental" will lead to positive physical changes. Remember, depression is a mind/body illness. Increasing the health of either of them will have a positive effect on the opposite system as well as the entire illness.

Mental Self-care and Coping

Learning how to analyze your thoughts:

In chapter 4 I talked about things like rumination, CBT, and the self-serving bias. These all fall under the category of conscious and unconscious thoughts. Our thoughts are some of the most powerful components to depression and likewise can have some of the most therapeutic effect on our moods.

Learning how to catch our thoughts and discovering what makes us feel bad is a huge help. It will help you when you're on your own (unless you're in a program most of your depression work will be done alone) and it will help any professionals you're working with. I cannot stress enough how important it is that you learn to listen to yourself. You will be surprised at what you discover. How we talk to ourselves has a huge impact on how we view the world. Learning how to break rumination cycles, pick up on self-harming negative thoughts, and turning those negative thoughts into positive one will be a huge help.

If the cause of your depression stems from thoughts like those listed, then becoming the master of your thoughts will go a long way towards lessening the effects of your depression. In order to help you, the exercises in Chapters 4 and 5 deal with these issues. So, if you're having problems with negative thinking I recommend you try the Analyzing your thoughts, Transforming Your Thoughts, and Breaking the Rumination Cycle exercises.

Low energy and motivation:

As you know, low energy and motivation are common effects of depression. You will have days when the world seems too big to take on and that bed is a much better option. You will fight with yourself because you know that you should be up and doing something...anything. It is on these days where baby steps are crucial. The following section has information and exercises you can try to help combat low energy and poor motivation.

Eliminating Distractions:

Distractions. They are all around us and fuel the human condition of wanting to be entertained. Learning how to eliminate distractions can be one of the most difficult strategies in learning how to be more productive. However, it is probably the strategy with the quickest and most noticeable results. Because as soon as the distraction(s) keeping you from accomplishing the task at hand are eliminated you will instantly feel more focused and ready to work.

Distractions will vary from person to person and they may be easy or difficult to identify. Things like the internet, food, TV, phones, and music are tangible things that we know are distractions. They're the things many of us go to when we're bored or just going through the routine. The intangible and internal distractions are the difficult ones to eliminate. These are the ones that can take time and concentrated effort to learn how to eliminate or ignore them.

Distractions that we can see are (for the most part) easy to remove. If you're bound to technology in some way, simply remove yourself from said technology. Turn the phone off, unplug the computer, or turn off the TV. Moving to another room away from the computer or TV is also effective. The world isn't going anywhere and will be there when you get back. Other times you may not have control over the distractions and it is necessary to remove yourself from the source. Going to another room or even an entirely different building might be necessary in some instances. A local library is a great place to go if you need some place quiet. A friend or relatives house is also a good option if you find yourself distracted by house work or something similar. It isn't possible for me to list every distraction and its solution.

Coping and Self-Care

Hopefully, I've given some general ideas that can applied to many different situations. And if not; come up with your own. Creating solutions to our own problems is a wonderful feeling.

Distractions outside of your body are most likely ones that everyone has dealt with at some point. The internal struggle that chronically depressed people deal with is something very few (fortunately) ever have to deal with. It is a personal battle that no two people can ever share. However, there are enough similarities that certain strategies can be implemented and tweaked to fit your situation. It is important to remember that internal conflict you feel, especially pertaining to focused effort, was a learned behavior. You were not born this way and it's possible to change how you think and feel about things. You may think what I'm going to suggest is stupid or it won't work. Trust me; I've been there. Sometimes it's easier to stay in a place that's comfortable even if it ends up hurting more.

Internal distractions are ones that we can't get away from. Things like warped perceptions, mood swings, low self-esteem etc...etc... The thoughts and feelings we have that seem to be a part of our personality.

This is where the true destructive power of depression comes from. The ability to change personalities is potent indeed. Even worse is that over time someone suffering from depression will begin to accept this new personality as their own. When someone reaches this point it is a struggle to regain what has been lost. In all honesty, they won't come out of it the same as they were before. All experience changes us and returning from the brink will have the same effect.

However, this doesn't mean that it is a bad thing. Successfully pulling yourself away from depression will give you an invaluable skill set that will help you the rest of your life. You will see life in a new light. This is why learning to eliminate or lessen the effects of internal distractions is so potent.

The only logical next step is to ask "how"? How do we eliminate these distractions which for right now make up a part of who we are? The first step comes from identifying your specific distractions. It would be impossible for me to list every single internal conflict you might have but, I've provided a short list of ones I feel are more common or easily relatable.

Anger

Low Self-Esteem

Loneliness

Fear

Anxiety

Annoyance

Irritability

Tired

Unmotivated

Unfocused

Anything going on internally that is keeping you from working can be added to this list. It doesn't matter how big or small you may think it is. If it's keeping you from making progress on something it needs to be addressed. If you're having trouble identifying your distraction(s) try this exercise.

Internal Conflict Exercise:

Tools needed: Paper and some kind of writing tool. Ten or fifteen minutes where you won't be interrupted.

Take your paper and turn it sideways so the long edges are top and bottom. At the top of the page write whatever it is that you want to do. Whatever it is that you want to achieve no matter how big or small. However you want to describe the activity is fine. If you only want to use one word or if you want to write a short sentence or paragraph. Anything works. Feel free to use as much of the paper as you need for the rest of the activity.

Once you have your first activity written down take a minute or two and imagine yourself trying to do the activity. I want you to focus on what kinds of feelings you experience. Specifically, the negative ones that are impeding your ability to get started. It's okay if you can't describe the feeling entirely. Just get a general idea because that is going to be the starting point. Once you have identified at least one of these distractions (you most likely will have more than one) skip a few lines on your paper and write down what that feeling is. Try to be as brief as possible. Once you've done this go back and search for any other obstacles you may have missed. If you find more write those underneath the activity in the same way that you did the first one. If you have more than one try and keep them evenly spaced on the paper.

Next draw a line between each feeling and the activity. The activity is what you want to achieve and the feelings you have listed are the surface thoughts stopping you from doing that activity. Now, go to the first emotion you wrote down and think about why you feel that way. How is that activity and that emotion linked? When you figure it out write it down underneath that emotion. Similar to the first part of the exercise, if you discover there is more than one reason write those down as well. Do this for each emotion linked to that activity.

Keep doing this cycle of linking thoughts to emotions until you feel that you have reached a root cause. Once you feel that you have found something stop. As with the core beliefs exercise we also have core disbeliefs.

Coping and Self-Care

Things that we believe to be true about the world, but aren't actually grounded in any kind of logic or reasoning. They are things we think are true and as such have worked themselves into who we are as a person. It is crucial to know how we truly think of ourselves in both a positive and negative light.

You now have a map of your thoughts. Depressed people usually have one of two types of thinking brain. The anxious brain that can't slow down and the sluggish suppressed brain that makes everything kind of look and feel the same. Some people experience both and others lean one way or the other. This activity allows you to save your thoughts on paper. You can come back to them at any time and retrace your steps. As you continue on your path to a better self you will probably come back and refine these thought maps. That's okay. Your first thought map may feel generalized which is fine. This isn't easy to do, especially if you're not used to this kind of self-awareness. As you get more practice, you will learn how to analyze yourself and can change your thought map whenever you like.

That's it. That is the exercise. There's no secret advice. No pressuring you to think about it positively. No way to magically make it disappear. As much as it isn't true about who you are as a person it is still in there. It's much like a knotted up ball of different colored yarn. You can't yank on the colors you want and expect to get them. It only makes the ball tighter. You have to be patient and work at the ball a little bit at a time. Undoing the knots and following the color you want in order to find out how to remove it properly. Our thoughts are the same way. It takes time, effort, patience, and the realization that you are worth the effort.

After you have completed the exercise, take that paper and put it somewhere you can look at it whenever you need to. Look at it on the bad days to remind yourself that whatever your feeling is not true. Chronically depressed people seem to have this ability to forget how they felt in the past and how they will feel in the future. The bad days feel as though the world will never be right again. On the good days we forget that we're even depressed. So use this paper to remind yourself that whatever you're feeling is not true and that you will have a good day again.

Simplify:

Life is complex. There is rarely a one size fits all solution to any given problem. For as many different problems there are one thousand and one ways to solve each of them. The same thing applies when we are attempting to enact change in our lives. For every activity or change there are many different ways to approach said change. To the chronically depressed person a complex task might be impossible. Trying to function can sap all of the willpower one may possess. When this willpower reserve is depleted, getting started on even the simplest tasks feels hopeless. For this reason, it is crucial to simplify things as much as possible.

Simplicity is oftentimes associated with something that is dumbed down, bad, or useless. Sometimes complexity is necessary. But, I find simplicity to be elegant. The simpler a task can be done or an idea explained the better. It is equally important for the depressed person because simple tasks and goals can oftentimes be easily achieved. It takes less energy and gives the added benefit of accomplishment. That positive feedback is what you need in order to keep going.

I am not saying that large or complex goals should not be attempted. It's perfectly fine to want to hike the Appalachian trail or visit every European country. I encourage you to dream big. But, if you have a hard time getting out of bed each day I think it's important to set yourself up for success first.

Don't feel like the small goals don't matter either. Depression tends to make everything significantly harder. Learn to celebrate the small victories in your everyday life. Feel great that you made it to work on time or that you picked up the house. You might say:

"Yea, but these are things we're supposed to do. They're expected of us."

To that I say yes, you are expected to do those things...if you're a normal functioning person. We are not normal function people and you should not expect yourself to act in a way conducive with that way of thinking. People with depression manage to push on and get things done even when every fiber of their being is telling them otherwise. That is amazing.

Simplifying tasks and goals will give you the boost you need to complete more of them. As you continue to work and improve yourself trying to accomplish bigger more complex tasks will happen naturally. But, we all have to start from somewhere. You don't start weight lifting by putting one hundred pounds on the bar. So, why should you try to do that with any other part of your life? Being chronically depressed requires that you start over and learn how to be productive again. Trying to pick things up from where you left off when you were in a good place is only going to frustrate you. Remember, simplicity for success.

If you're having trouble trying to simplify a task try this. Whatever it is that you are trying to do it should have some kind of measurable objective. It's most likely a certain amount of something. Probably a target time or a target quantity. Take that goal number and cut it in half. Cut it in half again. I want this number to be so small it will feel as though you aren't getting any benefit. This is your new goal number. When you do the task in question as soon as you reach that target number stop. Even if you feel like you can do more. Now feel good about yourself for reaching that goal.

For example, you might want to be able to walk or run for thirty minutes without stopping. Half of thirty is fifteen and half of that is seven and a half. So, for your first session your goal is seven and a half minutes. While this amount of time will not give you a lot of physical benefit (as far as exercise is concerned) the mental benefit of reaching your goal is important. Every time you go to walk or run add one or two minutes to that seven and a half minute time. It doesn't take many sessions after that to reach your original goal of thirty minutes.

$30 - 7.5 = 22.5$

That is how many sessions you would need at a one minute increase per session. At three sessions a week it would only take seven weeks to reach that goal. Which is only a little less than two months.

The second part of this is to start keeping a journal tracking your progress. Whenever you do this task record how much you completed. Every time you do this task try and add a little more. Don't go crazy. You still want this number to be low enough so you can reach your goal. Keep adding each time until you reach your original target number. It may seem silly but I promise you will reach your goal in less time than you think.

Using this idea of simplicity can be a powerful tool in combating the demotivating factors associated with depression. Learning to feel good about completing goals (no matter how small they are) will go a long way.

The Problem of Happiness:

I've included this in the coping section because I feel it is a question that those of us with depression ask ourselves. What is happiness? What will make me happy? It is a difficult question and one that I don't have a definite answer. But, I've done my best to answer the problem of happiness in a way that makes sense to me. These are my thoughts about the issue and hopefully you can find some solace in my explanation or at least a starting point to do your own introspection about the topic.

I don't how other cultures view happiness, but I feel confident in saying that America has it wrong. Happiness is supposed to be a feeling. An emotion. Something that is not infinite. Yet, that's what so many people strive to achieve. They want to be happy all the time. We get told by popular media and culture that if we aren't happy then we aren't doing something right. And those in the marketing field know this. They use it to their advantage when trying to sell products. Whatever they're trying to sell is going to improve your life in some way and make you happier. Having all this sunshine and rainbows shoved down our throats warps our world view. Many Americans believe that they are supposed to be happy constantly. This is impossible.

The first and probably most important part in beginning to understand happiness is that we cannot physiologically be happy all the time. The human body strives for something called homeostasis. "Homeostasis is the property of a system in which variables are regulated so that internal conditions remain stable and relatively constant". (19) This basically means that whatever system you are talking about, when everything is in balance, then homeostasis has been achieved. We tend to use the word when describing biological functions. If you feel no hunger, no thirst, and feel safe, then you are described as being in homeostasis. We can apply the same idea to emotions as well.

Every person has a baseline emotional state. This will differ between individuals. But, it is a state that I describe as content or neutral. This balanced state of emotion is what we should all strive to achieve. Happiness is simply one part of our emotional range. Similar to how we don't want to be angry, sad, or fearful all of the time, we should also not want to be happy all of the time. It is an emotional state that is to be experienced in short duration.

We tend to think of happiness as a positive emotion, which is true. It can give us a boost of energy, confidence, creativity, or the lift in mood we need to get through the day. However, experiencing happiness all of the time is not conducive to emotional well-being. We need to experience the negative emotions and lows of life as well. I feel that this is important for a variety of reasons, but is outside the scope of this book. There are philosophical as well as psychological papers and texts on the subject. My reason for bringing this topic up is to help give a better idea of the kind of emotional state you should be striving to attain.

When we are told that we're more or less broken if we aren't happy all the time, it gets to be discouraging for those of us who have a hard time simply not feeling sad. I'm here to tell you that a constant state of happiness is not what you should be trying to achieve. It is an impossible state of being to have and creates a scenario for failure. This idea of neutrality or evenness is a better emotional state to try and achieve.

I think it is important to keep this in mind when trying to get out of a depressive state. It's important to remember that even though we want to be happy again, it isn't this state of euphoria that our culture tries to make it out to be. Look at any day that you feel less down as a victory. It's one day you beat the illness. You won't win all the time, but eventually, as you learn how to handle chronic depression, you will have more good days than bad ones. So in closing, don't fall for the trap of "I need to be happy all the time to feel normal". Happiness is one part of a complex emotional array and should be treated as such. You can feel happiness again. Remember that when you come down from it you aren't crashing into a depressive episode. We must return to the baseline of our emotional state. So enjoy the happiness when it comes, but don't latch onto it or be fearful that it will never return. Depression and sadness are simply the opposite of happiness. We need both in order to experience each. So appreciate happiness, but remember that it is not the ideal emotional state.

Self-care is an important part of your depression treatment and should not be overlooked. You must be an active participant and work on things outside of professional treatment. There are a variety of ways to do this and whichever ones you choose are entirely up to you. As long as it works for you and you can make it a habit. Consistency is the most important part of doing self-care. You must think it's working and that you're getting something out of the activity. If you only take away one thing from this chapter make it consistency. Sticking with something will take you far as you continue to progress in your recovery.

Chapter 8
Resources

This chapter is a compilation of resources I have used, and others that I think will be useful to you. It is a selection of books, websites, and phone numbers. Some of them are here to cover concepts and ideas I've talked about in more depth and others are tools to help you find professional resources. None of them are a requirement, but all will be helpful in one way or another.

Phone Numbers:

Adolescent Suicide Hotline:

800-621-4000

Drug & Alcohol Treatment Hotline:

Resources

800-662-HELP (4357)

Help Finding a Therapist:

1-800-THERAPIST (1-800-843-7274)

National Alliance on Mental Illness (NAMI):

1-800-950-NAMI (6264)

Sexual Assault Hotline:

1-800-656-4673

Suicide Prevention Lifeline:

1-800-273-TALK (8255)

Suicide & Crisis Hotline:

1-800-999-9999

Suicide Prevention – The Trevor HelpLine:

(Specializing in gay and lesbian youth suicide prevention)

1-800-850-8078

Websites:

This first batch of sites are all professionally run mental health organizations. They will give you a lot of information about mental illness, medications, getting help paying for treatment, and where you can find help.

American Academy of Child and Adolescent Psychiatry: http://www.aacap.org/

American Psychiatric Association: http://www.psychiatry.org/

American Psychological Association: http://www.apa.org/

American Society for Adolescent Psychiatry: http://adolescent-psychiatry.org/

American Society for Clinical Psychopharmacology: http://www.ascpp.org/

Brain & Behavior Research Foundation: https://bbrfoundation.org/

Depression and Bipolar Support Alliance: http://www.dbsalliance.org/

Mental Health America: http://www.nmha.org/

National Alliance on Mental Illness: http://www.nami.org/

Psychology today: https://www.psychologytoday.com/

Specifically the Find a Therapist tab.

MoodGym: https://moodgym.anu.edu.au/welcome

Resources

Free online course that will teach you about Cognitive Behavioral Therapy and walk you through the steps of applying it to your life.

BlahTherapy: http://blahtherapy.com/

Find a therapist or simply a stranger to talk to. Therapists have a rate and strangers can be talked to for free 24/7.

7 Cups: http://www.7cups.com/

Trained volunteer listeners in text format.

Meetup: http://www.meetup.com/

Find a variety of social clubs and meet ups in your area.

Healthy Place: http://www.healthyplace.com/depression/depression-treatment/gold-standard-for-treating-depression-toc/

Links to articles and videos dealing with all parts of depression.

Wing of Madness: http://www.wingofmadness.com/

One of the oldest blogs about depression on the internet. Has articles, advice, and book recommendations.

Books:

The books I have listed below will cover topics on nutrition, exercise, and areas of psychology I think are helpful when dealing with chronic depression.

Practical Programming for Strength Training 3rd Edition: by Mark Rippetoe & Andy Baker

Stretching: by Bob Anderson

Convict Conditioning: How to Bust Free of All Weakness--Using the Lost Secrets of Supreme Survival Strength: by Paul Wade

Convict Conditioning 2: Advanced Prison Training Tactics for Muscle Gain, Fat Loss, and Bulletproof Joints: By Paul Wade

Eat to Live: The Amazing Nutrient-Rich Program for Fast and Sustained Weight Loss, Revised Edition: by Joel Fuhrman, MD

Whole: Rethinking the Science of Nutrition: by T. Colin Cmpbell, PhD and Howard Jacobson, PhD

The China Study: The Most Comprehensive Study of Nutrition Ever Conducted And the Startling Implications for Diet, Weight Loss, And Long-term Health1st Edition: by T. Colin Campbell, PhD and Thomas M. Campbel II. MD

Self Esteem Third Edition: by Matthew McKay, PH.D and Patrick Fanning

Mindsight: by Daniel J. Siegel

Resources

Living well with depression and Bipolar disorder: What Your Doctor Doesn't Tell you…That You Need to Know by John McManamy

The Depression Cure: by Stephen S. Ilardi, PhD

Making Habits, Breaking Habits: Why We Do Things, Why We Don't, and How to Make Any Change Stick by Jeremy Dean

Get It Done When You're Depressed: by Julie A. Fas and John D. Preston, Psy.D., ABPP

Why Zebras Don't Get Ulcers, Third Edition: by Robert M. Sapolsky

Conclusion

Chronic depression is undeniably a condition that requires lifestyle changes. You have to be more attentive to your thoughts, surroundings, and choices. Every day there is the possibility of ending up on a path towards a major depressive episode. This is something you will deal with for the rest of your life. I believe that people who end up with recurring depression will struggle with it their whole lives. However, that doesn't mean everyday will be hard. Some symptoms can be managed and reduced. Others can be eliminated entirely. Making life work with this illness is part balancing act and part self-knowledge.

It's impossible to identify every event or thought that leads to depression. This is a highly personal illness. Every person who experiences depression will have a

Conclusion

different angle on the illness. Yes, there will be similarities and common ground upon which people with PDD can stand. But, it's the individuality of the illness that can make it so difficult to treat. It's why at every stage of your treatment you have to do what works for you.

Not everything I've written will resonate with you. Some of it you may disagree with. That's okay. I didn't set out with the goal to end every depressed person's suffering (although that would be nice). I'm sharing my experience and knowledge with you in an attempt to create curiosity. I want you to use this book as a resource, a kind of guide. Something you can turn to when you're stuck and need some new ideas.

Ultimately, your treatment is up to you. You are the one that has to truly want to get better. It will be scary, frustrating and filled with setbacks. It will also be filled with joy, successes, and intense knowledge about who you are as an individual. This illness makes you take a hard look at yourself. By doing that you learn a little more about humanity. You learn how to relate people on a deep level. You learn about true compassion because you know about suffering.

That's one of the interesting things about this disease. The two sidedness of everything. You slowly learn the good things that can come from it while also hating what it has done to you. I must be clear, I am not attempting to romanticize depression in any way. It is a terrible disease that destroys people. However, it's also a transformative experience. You would have to be some supernatural entity to not go through depression and change in some way. It changes the way you look at the world and interact with people. Some days negatively and others positively. Given enough time, patience, and work those positive changes will begin to outweigh the bad ones.

Having lived with depression for so long (at least 11 years when I wrote this) I can actually say I like the person depression has caused me to become. I understand that a lot of you reading this will think I'm crazy. But, if you work at it and understand things can be better, I'm confident you will understand what I'm talking about one day. It's not easy and it took me a long time. And my hope in writing this book is that I can help you along your way. I want you to come to a place of acceptance. To place where you can say that you're happy with who you are as an individual. Where you understand that imperfection is okay and that there are other people who know what you're going through. I want you to almost come to peace with depression and understand that there's not necessarily something wrong with you. Only that you experience life in a way that often leads to pain and suffering.

But once you understand this, and I mean truly understand it, this illness called depression loses its power over you. Of course you will still have some symptoms

Conclusion

and it will always require management and work (I still have many bad moments, days, and weeks). But this isn't the end. I know it may feel like nothing will get better and that treatment is hopeless. I honestly understand that feeling. There is hope however. With enough work and self-care you will get better. It would be impossible for you not to get better. Unfortunately, I can't give you a time line for when that will happen. As many ways as there are to fall into depression there are as many ways to recover from depression.

All I ask of you, who has read this book in an effort to rid yourself if your disease, is to give things time. Practice every day, learn about yourself, and be patient. Chronic depression is not the end for you. In fact I feel like the amount of recovery I've been able to achieve has only deepened my love for life. I sincerely hope the same thing happens for you.

A Small Thank You

Thank you for reading my book. It means a lot that you took a chance on an independently published book. Especially one about such a heavy topic. If you're struggling with depression I hope that you got something out of my experience. If you're reading this for someone else, I hope this has been an enlightening read for you. It was certainly an adventure writing this and I plan to write more in the future (not quite sure about what though). Once again, thank you so much for your support.

About the Author

Gabriel Reisinger is a writer who has struggled with depression for most of his teen and adult life. He currently enjoys fitness, nutrition, psychology, philosophy, and a number of other subjects. He hopes to continue his writing career and would like to someday provide therapy for individuals struggling with mood disorders.

Notes:

1. Depressive Disorders. (2013). In Diagnostic and Statistical Manual of Mental Disorders (Fifth ed., p. 168). Arlington, Virginia: American Psychiatric Publishing.

2. "Dysthymic Disorder Among Adults." NIMH RSS. Web. 16 Oct. 2015.
<http://www.nimh.nih.gov/health/statistics/prevalence/dysthymic-disorder-among-adults.shtml>.

3. "What Causes Depression? - Harvard Health." Harvard Health. Web. 16 Oct. 2015.
<http://www.health.harvard.edu/mind-and-mood/what-causes-depression>.

4. "THE BRAIN FROM TOP TO BOTTOM." THE BRAIN FROM TOP TO BOTTOM. Web. 16 Oct. 2015.

<http://the-brain.mcgill.ca/flash/a/a_08/a_08_cr/a_08_cr_dep/a_08_cr_dep.html>.

5. "Understanding Addiction.": How Addiction Hijacks the Brain. Web. 16 Oct. 2015. <http://www.helpguide.org/harvard/how-addiction-hijacks-the-brain.htm>.

6. Merriam-Webster. Merriam-Webster. Web. 16 Oct. 2015. <http://www.merriam-webster.com/dictionary/stress>.

7. McKay, Matthew, and Martha Davis.Thoughts & Feelings: Taking Control of Your Moods and Your Life. 2nd ed. Oakland, CA: New Harbinger Publications, 1997. Print.

8. "Rumination(psychology)."Wikipedia. Wikimedia Foundation. Web. 30 Oct. 2015.

9. Fanning, Patrick, and Matthew McKay, PhD. "The Pathological Critic."Self-esteem: Third Edition.Oakland: New Harbinger Publicaions, 2000. 15. Print.

10. Beck, Judith S., and Judith S. Beck. "Evaluating Automatic Thoughts."Cognitive Behavior Therapy: Basics and beyond. 2nd ed. New York: Guilford, 2011. 181-182. Print.

11. Dean, Jeremy. "Birth of a Habit."Making Habits, Breaking Habits: Why We Do Things, Why We Don't,

Notes

and How to Make Any Change Stick. Boston: Da Capo, 2013. 13. Print.

12. "Habit." Dictionary.com. Dictionary.com. Web. 2 Nov. 2015.

13. Habits in everyday life: Thought, emotion, and action.

Wood, Wendy; Quinn, Jeffrey M.; Kashy, Deborah A.

Journal of Personality and Social Psychology, Vol 83(6), Dec 2002, 1281-1297.

14. Oettingen, G. "Future Thought and Behaviour Change." European Review of Social Psychology 23, no. 1 (2012): 1-63.

15. Gollwitzer, P. M. (1999). Implementation intentions: Strong effects of simple plans. American Psychologist, 54, 493-503.

16. Lambert, Gw, C. Reid, Dm Kaye, Gl Jennings, and Md Esler. "Effect of Sunlight and Season on Serotonin Turnover in the Brain." The Lancet360.9348: 1840-842.NCBI. Web. 19 Nov. 2015.

17. Gangwisch, J. E., L. Hale, L. Garcia, D. Malaspina, M. G. Opler, M. E. Payne, R. C. Rossom, and D. Lane. "High Glycemic Index Diet as a Risk Factor for Depression: Analyses from the Women's Health Initiative." American Journal of Clinical Nutrition102.2 (2015):

454-63.The American Journal of Clinical Nutrition. Web. 24 Nov. 2015.

18. Kross, E., M. G. Berman, W. Mischel, E. E. Smith, and T. D. Wager. "Social Rejection Shares Somatosensory Representations with Physical Pain."Proceedings of the National Academy of Sciences108.15 (2011): 6270-275.Proceedings of the National Academy of Sciences of the United States of America. Web. 24 Nov. 2015.

19. (n.d.). Retrieved November 29, 2015, from https://en.wikipedia.org/wiki/Homeostasis

Index

A

Accountability partner, 34

Amygdala, 47, 52
    Fear response, 47

Anhedonia, 17

C

Chronic Depression, 31

Chronic Major Depressive Disorder, 14

Clinical Treatment, 118

Core Beliefs, 67

Counselor, 121-123

D

Depression Support, 32

Diagnostic and Statistical Manual of Mental Disorders, 13

Diet, 142-146

Distractions, 152-156

DSM, 13, 14, 15

Dysthymia, 14

E

Early onset, 23

Episodic, 19-20

Exercise, 137-140

F

Friends and family, 147-148

G

Grief, 17

Guilt, 17

H

Habits, 20-21, 97-103

    Appraisal, 108

    Creating, 106-108

    Depression, 103-106

Happiness, 163-168

Hippocampus, 46

Homeostasis, 46, 164

Hypothalamus, 46

    CRH, 46

    Stressor, 46

    Vasopressin, 46

I

Implementation Intention, 112

    If, 112-113

    Then, 113-114

Inpatient, 131-132

Internal conflict, 154-156

L

Late onset, 23

Low energy, 152

Luxury depression facility, 132

M

Major Depression, 24

Major Depressive Episode, 24

Medication, 123-124

    Atypical, 126

    MAOI, 128

    SSRI, 125

    Tricyclic, 127-128

Mindfulness, 104

Index

Mistakes of Thinking, 89–92

Motivation, 63–65

N

Negative Thought Patterns, 70–72

Neurotransmitters, 48–50

    Dopamine, 52–53

    Norepinephrine, 51

    Serotonin, 50–51

O

Online, 148–149

P

Partial programs, 131

Persistent Depressive Disorder, 13, 14, 24

    Requirements, 15

PDD, 13, 24, 29

    Symptoms 15–20, 31

PHP, 131

Professional Help, 35, 118

Psychomotor retardation, 18–19

Psychologist, 120, 121

Psychiatrist, 120, 121

Q

Questionnaire, 26–27

R

Resources, 167

    Books, 170–172

    Phone, 167–168

    Websites, 168–170

Ruminating, 81–82

S

Self-esteem, 86–89

Self-care, 135

    Mental, 151

    Physical, 136

Self-harm, 18

Chronic Depression: A User's Manual

Self-serving bias, 84-85, 108

Simplify, 159-163

Socializing, 41-42

Social clubs, 150-151

Social interaction, 146-147

Social worker, 121

Stress, 24-25, 54-55

    Alarm, 56-57

    Chemical, 55-56

    Emotional, 56

    Exhaustion, 57-58

    Physical, 53-54

    Resistance, 57

    Response, 53

    Symptoms, 24-25

Sunshine, 136-137

Support network, 32

Therapy, 34, 120

Thoughts,

    Accepting, 79-81

    Analyze, 72, 151-152

    Distress 75-74

    Create 78-79

    Transform, 75

    Valid, 76-78

Treatment programs, 130

T

Therapist, 34

    Finding one, 37-38

Printed in Great Britain
by Amazon